The Evergreens

Leucothoë editorum, "DROOPING LEUCOTHE"

The Evergreens

by James H. Beale

ILLUSTRATED WITH PHOTOGRAPHS

DOUBLEDAY & COMPANY, INC., 1960

GARDEN CITY, NEW YORK

Preface

The constantly increasing mileage of landscaped parkways, a more enlightened public appreciation of municipal and state parks and of the need for the preservation of large unspoiled areas of natural beauty for the benefit of a rapidly growing population, added to the increasing use of trees and shrubs in the beautification of civic projects, have all helped to focus the attention of the average citizen on the desirability of the greater use of this form of living material in the improvement of his surroundings. With the vastly increased number of homeowners this, in turn, has prompted a sharpening of interest and attention on that smaller area where the individual holds control and must decide what constitutes appropriateness with beauty—his or her own garden.

In the following pages it is hoped the reader may find assistance in making decisions about one group of plants, the evergreen trees and shrubs, of the several that must be included in a well-furnished garden. Trees and shrubs, whether evergreen or deciduous, are permanent, living occupants of the ground and should improve with the years, and it is a little surprising that in the past they so often have been taken for granted, with little or no assistance toward developing their full beauty, and not infrequently with only a very hazy idea even of their kind.

Fortunately, for some time this attitude has been slowly undergoing a change. More and more homeowners are taking a genuine interest in the plants they grow, and are no longer content to use only "run of the mill" material that is constantly repeated in every suburban and country development. This last statement, however, is not intended in any way to belittle the many quite common but nevertheless beautiful plants that are indispensable to any garden of charm. It would be ridiculous to suggest that, in order to be different from one's neighbors, a garden be devoted to plants curious merely because they are uncommon, to those with very little eye appeal, or entirely to those near the border line of hardiness, as the latter might be quite unsightly after the storms of an average winter and really tragic in appearance after one of more than normal severity. But when the correct growing conditions can be provided, there are many evergreens worthy of more extended trial even though they may not flaunt their beauty with the extravagance of some more familiar kinds.

It is impossible to give the exact geographical locations in this country in which the plants mentioned herein may be grown. As a broad guide it may be taken to include the Cape Cod area of Massachusetts, and southward east of the Allegheny Mountains to South Carolina, and westward in the cooler portions of some of the Gulf and nearby states to the north of them with similar climate and rainfall. Not by any means, however, are all of the plants mentioned to be expected to grow in the whole of that area, but further information on this point is given with the plants. Excellent advice may also be obtained from local

6

nurserymen and garden clubs, from state experiment stations and county agricultural agents, and anyone wishing more detailed botanical information about plants they may be considering should consult Alfred Rehder's *Manual of Cultivated Trees and Shrubs,* and Liberty Hyde Bailey's *Cyclopedia of Horticulture,* or *Hortus Second.*

A word about the way in which this book is arranged may be helpful. Following the cultural chapters, the conifers, the broadleaved evergreens, and the Heath family are given in separate chapters, and for easy reference the plants in each of these groups are in the alphabetical sequence of the genus to which they belong. The name of the botanical family in which a genus occurs is centered above the genus.

As noted above, the plants of the Heath family, the *Ericaceae,* are given a chapter to themselves, and it will be immediately obvious to many readers that this treatment is inconsistent, as the Heath family is merely a part of the larger broad-leaved group, and its various genera should, therefore, be alphabetically dispersed throughout the latter group. But because of the number of plants it contains, many of which are among the choicer ornamentals, and of their usually rather special cultural requirements, it seemed better to make it an exception and devote a chapter to it.

Some of the commoner botanical synonyms that are still in frequent use in place of currently accepted botanical names are given in parentheses.

Finally, to my friend of many, many years, Montague Free, my sincere thanks for the many suggestions he made, for reading the manuscript, and for suggesting I undertake it. Also to my wife, for the patience and time she devoted to the more uninteresting part of its preparation.

James H. Beale

Contents

Illustrations

13

14

The Evergreens

1 The Two Groups of Evergreens

Hardy evergreen trees and shrubs may be divided into two groups; the narrow-leaved evergreens or conifers, and the broad-leaved evergreens. It is unnecessary to go into the differences between these two groups in any detail, but some of the broader distinctions may be indicated.

To begin with the conifers—the leaves of many plants of this group are commonly referred to as "needles" because they are extremely narrow in proportion to their length. This is readily seen in such familiar examples as Pine, *Pinus*, Fir, *Abies*, and Spruce, *Picea*. In *Podocarpus* an exception to this rule occurs, for here the leaves are much broader and have little resemblance to the leaves of most conifers, but the kinds of *Podocarpus* are not sufficiently hardy for northern gardens, though some are much favored for almost frost-free areas of southern and western states.

In some other kinds of conifer, however, the leaves are exceedingly small and scale-like, densely crowded and overlap-

17

ping on the shoots, and quite unlike those of the plants named above. Examples of this kind of conifer are Arborvitae, *Thuja*, False-cypress, *Chamaecyparis,* and Juniper, *Juniperus,* though in the last-named genus some species have needle- or awl-like leaves, others have scale-like leaves, or both may be present. However, in Arborvitae, False-cypress, and Juniper, awl-like leaves are normal to the seedling or juvenile stage of the plants, and some of their varieties retain this type of foliage, but except in some Junipers it normally gives way to the mature type, which is, as already stated, scale-like.

The flowers of conifers, when compared to those of many of the broad-leaved evergreens, are comparatively inconspicuous and never white or brightly colored. The pistillate (female) and staminate (male) flowers occur separately on the same or on different plants, but in the latter case they are, of course, plants of the same kind or species. Conifer flowers have little similarity to the common idea of flowers. The pollen-bearing staminate flowers are much like catkins in appearance, and the usually abundant pollen is carried by wind to the pistillate flowers. The latter are small cones which in their early stages are not always readily detected.

The conifers receive this name from the fact that the fruits or seed-bearing vessels of many of them are usually some sort of cone, a word so well understood it requires little explanation. Briefly, a cone is made up of scales varying in number, shape, and size with the kind of conifer that bears it. The scales are formed around a central axis, overlap, and follow a definite pattern in their arrangement. In most instances cones are more or less woody at maturity, and the scales separate to release the seeds which have developed at their bases.

Cones vary considerably in size, again according to the kind of conifer, from the half-inch length of some of the Arborvitaes to the five- or six- or occasionally ten-inch length of those of the White Pine, *Pinus Strobus*, of the eastern states, though the cones of some western Pines are still larger. Cone size, however, is not related to size of tree, as the cones of the most massive, and what, until recently, were believed to be the oldest living things on earth, the Giant Sequoias or Big Trees, *Sequoiadendron*, of California, are only two or three inches long, while those of the Sugar Pine, *Pinus Lambertiana*, which, though a magnificent tree, does not approach the bulk of the Giant Sequoia, may be twenty inches long.

Cones are usually green while they are immature, and in this stage are not conspicuous against the green foliage unless they are in great numbers or seen at close range. There are differences of opinion about the decorative quality of the many kinds which turn brown at maturity. In the immature stage the cones of many Firs are distinctly more ornamental than those of most other hardy conifers because they are usually purplish in color and stand erect on the branches. Juniper fruits are berry-like though they also are cones, but with fleshy scales which grow together to form a berry, and do not become woody and separate when mature as is the more normal habit of cones.

A contrast occurs in plants of the Yew family, *Taxaceae*, some of which have plum-like fruits, and, others, seeds partly enclosed in a fleshy coat, and of the latter the best-known examples are the Yews, *Taxus*. Yews produce their fruits singly on the shoots, and each seed is surrounded by a fleshy red aril or coat open at the top exposing part of the seed. These seeds, but not the arils, are poisonous to man and livestock, but birds relish the arils and void the seeds undigested.

In the absence of cones—and often these are not produced for many years—the principal distinction between the broad-leaved and narrow-leaved evergreens is in the foliage, though there are instances where superficial examination may be misleading.

Coming now to the broad-leaved evergreens—not all of these have conspicuous or decorative flowers, so it is impossible to separate the two groups simply on this feature. Broad-leaved evergreens most frequently have the pistillate and staminate organs in the same flower, though, as in the conifers, the flowers of one sex may be on different plants from those of the opposite sex, or again the sexes may be in different flowers on the same plant. However, a plant can usually be assigned to one group or the other with reasonable certainty from its foliage characters even though its name is not known.

Unlike the conifers the broad-leaved evergreens follow no common patterns in leaf shape or uniformity of flowers or fruits. Leaves range in size from the tiny ones of Heather, *Calluna,* to the large size of those of some Rhododendrons. Flowers may be as colorful as in these two examples or as unimposing as those of Japanese Holly, *Ilex crenata,* or Box, *Buxus,* but it is extremely unlikely anyone would deny either of the latter a place in the garden because of its lack of showy flowers. Fruits may be utterly devoid of interest from a decorative point of view, or as striking as those of American Holly, *Ilex opaca,* or Firethorn, *Pyracantha.*

2 Hardiness in Evergreens

It is often impossible to say with assurance what plants, other than local natives, will be hardy in a region. Hardiness can be taken to mean the ability to withstand winter cold, but as is shown later, some unusual climatic conditions, such as a prolonged drought during the previous year, or occasionally as the cumulative effect of a succession of such years, may have a pronounced effect on the ability of plants to pass through a winter without injury. Excessive as well as insufficient amounts of water in the soil, or of atmospheric moisture, or of shade or exposure are all factors influencing hardiness.

The observant plantsman who is growing a wide variety of plants soon realizes there are some odd contradictions, both pleasing and disappointing, to what he may have anticipated in the matter of hardiness. When deciding to grow plants about which there is no local information, it is advisable to learn as much as possible about them before assuming they will prove entirely satisfactory in a new environment.

Widely different conditions affect a plant's ability to withstand the rigors of winter, particularly in the northeastern portion of this country, even though it occurs in the climatic zone generously designated as "temperate." Low temperatures more or less sustained, sudden changes in temperature and gales often accompanied by sleet-, ice-, or snowstorms are the ordinary conditions of winter to which every woody-stemmed plant growing in the open is exposed. Severe as the elements are to the naked branches of deciduous trees and shrubs, it is not difficult to appreciate how much more severe they must be to the much greater area of surface exposed to their influence by the foliage of broad-leaved and coniferous evergreens.

Over long periods of time the evergreens native to any region have adapted themselves to their environment, but this adaptability varies considerably, for some kinds are dispersed over wide ranges of country and climate while others are restricted to comparatively limited areas.

Those broad-leaved evergreens native to the high mountain and extreme northern regions of the world are low in stature, and for many months each year are protected from the injurious effects of very low temperatures by the most efficient of all protective winter coverings, a cover of snow. Near the altitudinal or latitudinal timber lines of their range, some of the hardiest conifers are dwarfed to a degree that sometimes has led to the assumption that they were of a different kind than the larger examples of the same plant found in more favorable parts of the range.

Further southward, and increasingly so at lower elevations where winter conditions become less severe, the kinds of broad-leaved evergreens multiply in number, and many in size, until in sub-tropical and tropical regions they become commonplace as large shrubs or trees.

22

Evergreens of northern regions require a resting period, however, and this coincides with the winter months. For those whose range extends considerably south it is often of sufficient length only at increasingly higher and cooler elevations in the mountains, though the northern edge of their range may be near sea level. But the greater rainfall in the mountains may be as essential to some of them as the cooler temperature. Some North American native plants may occasionally be injured in regions where they are assumed to be perfectly hardy, when any weather condition or peculiar combination of conditions deviates from those ordinarily experienced.

It is not common practice, however, to grow in gardens only those plants which are native to the region. Professional and amateur plant collectors have introduced others from every part of the world having a climate remotely similar to any part of this vast country. There is always the possibility that such introductions will prove adaptable to a change of environment, and that some feature they possess be sufficiently distinct from other plants in cultivation to add beauty and interest to American gardens.

It is wrong to assume, however, that plants of foreign origin are necessarily superior to the many excellent natives which have proved their decorative value for gardens, though it is probably still true that a number of the latter are more highly prized in Europe than in this land of their origin. But the addition of introductions from other lands provides a much wider choice of material. Therefore, as a general rule, plants should be selected on their merits for the purpose for which they are intended without regard to their place of origin but with due thought to their suitability to the climate and soil in which they are to be grown.

It should not be surprising when some of these introductions do not behave with the tolerance of local natives, but rather that so many of them have proved amenable to changed conditions. Unless gardening is to become static this system of trial and error must continue, but the areas of the world which have not been thoroughly explored for suitable hardy plants are becoming very limited. Few would deny that the rewards in satisfaction have more than justified many past introductions. Who would care to see their gardens suddenly deprived of such familiar European plants as English Ivy, Box, Austrian Pine, or Norway Spruce, and from the other side of the world, such entrenched favorites as Pachysandra, or Japanese Holly and Japanese Yew, to mention a mere handful. China's contribution is enormous, and the late E. H. Wilson very appropriately recognized this in one of his books, *China, Mother of Gardens.*

Many plants of foreign origin succeed so well that their hardiness is accepted without question until freakish winter weather leaves its mark on them or some factor other than weather has made them susceptible to winter injury. It is not only the place of origin which may be the reason for a plant's susceptibility to injury, but conditions in its immediate vicinity may be responsible.

The kind and condition of the soil are among these limitations. Because clay soils, commonly known as "heavy" soils, retain more moisture than those of a lighter, more sandy nature, they tend, in a normal year, to cause active growth to continue later into the fall than is desirable, consequently there is always the possibility that plant tissues will not be so fully ripened as is necessary if they are to avoid winter injury. Much the same condition may arise in any soil not adequately drained. Similarly, abnormally wet weather in late summer may be responsible for an undue prolongation of the growing season. Excessive use of fertilizers, or their use late in the season while plants are still actively growing, is another factor contributing to winter injury by causing growth to continue beyond its normal period. Early spring is the most suitable time to apply fertilizers to evergreens, and usually no later than early June.

The reverse of the above conditions occurs when winter injury is the result of excessive spring and summer drought, or of insufficient rainfall late in the year. Unless evergreens contain a normal supply of water when they enter that period of the year when the ground is deeply frozen for a long time, the smaller amount they contain may be dangerously depleted by transpiration, as the roots are unable to draw water from the frozen soil to replace the loss. Most hardy plants are equipped to withstand some loss under normal conditions, but when the winter is severe and prolonged the loss is much greater, particularly in broad-leaved evergreens, than can be compensated for by any natural means.

A sudden, violent drop in temperature in early winter, before vegetation has had time to become hardened to the degree that occurs later in the winter, is an occasional cause of serious injury. But a similar drop a couple of months later may have little adverse effect, though it sometimes destroys flower buds. Exposure to winter winds, usually most damaging from the North or Northwest, often results in severe "burning" or partial defoliation of broad-leaved evergreens, and of some conifers, and a barrier against wind is often essential. Trees of the White Pine, *Pinus Strobus,* a perfectly hardy native, may be severely "burned" by winter wind and are quite unsightly until the injury is hidden by new growth.

A barrier of hardy trees and shrubs is the best protection from wind, but temporary shelters such as are suggested in Chapter 4 may suffice. Or the formation of the land may channel the wind from another direction into some part of the garden with such constancy that it has the same damaging effect as when it originates in a colder quarter. And wind coming round the corner of a building and directed onto one or more plants may be the cause of severe injury or death to them, while similar plants in a more open situation are unharmed.

Air drainage may have as important results in reference to winter hardiness as soil drainage. Cold air sinks to the lowest possible level, and on sloping ground on still nights the cold upper air rolls down the slope to take the place of the lighter, rising warm air, and there it remains until wind or an increase in temperature by means of sun heat dispels it. For this reason gardens in the bottom of valleys usually experience more injury than those on the hillsides. The lower location is not only the coldest, but frost strikes there earlier in autumn and later in spring than at higher levels. Whenever there is a choice of positions, doubtfully hardy plants should be planted on the slope, and not at its base. It is a common experience to find that of two plants of the same kind the one planted in the lower position is injured more frequently or more severely than the one on the higher ground, which may escape all injury.

Plants recently set out are more subject to winter injury than those well established in the soil, and small ones usually more so than larger ones of the same kind without regard to when they were planted. Severe insect injury or disease may undermine the vitality of plants to such an extent that they are further weakened or killed by winter weather.

Shade is another factor having considerable bearing upon the winter hardiness of many broad-leaved evergreens. The amount of shade may be no more than is cast by the bare branches of nearby deciduous trees, but is sufficient to modify the intensity of sunlight and allow for the more gradual thawing of frozen tissues. Japanese Andromeda, *Pieris japonica,* when fully exposed to winter sunlight, is often disappointing in spring because of the absence of flowers. The flower buds are formed during the previous summer and are a prominent feature of the plants all winter, but constantly repeated freezing and thawing may kill them, while other plants provided with light shade will bloom profusely.

A similar kind of injury may occur in hybrid Rhododendrons following a winter of more than usual severity. If all the flowers within the protecting bud scales are not killed, fewer than the normal number emerge in spring and close inspection will reveal many small, blackened buds around the base of those which survived. Oregon Holly-grape, *Mahonia Aquifolium,* when planted in shade is one of the most satisfactory evergreens, but in the sun the foliage is almost invariably injured to such an extent as to be an eyesore until new growth hides it.

On the other hand, the density of shade may be so great that evergreens which are grown principally for their flowers may be almost total failures in that respect. This can happen when they are planted beneath low-branched deciduous trees which provide ample protection in winter, but in summer when the trees are in leaf the evergreens do not receive sufficient light to develop flower buds. Many of the broad-leaved evergreens grow well and blossom freely when planted on the north side of buildings, provided they are protected from northerly winds and there is no overhead shade. But heavy overhead shade in such a location, usually caused by the overhanging branches of trees in the near vicinity, will result in thin growth and an almost total lack of flower-bud formation because of insufficient light. Under the latter conditions, however, the roots of the trees responsible for the excessive shade must sometimes bear part of the blame, as they impoverish the soil of moisture and fertility. Conifers, with very few exceptions, require ample sunlight to develop fully their decorative qualities.

A long period of very low temperatures is probably responsible for the most extensive winter injury, especially when accompanied by much sunny weather and high, dry winds. Under these circumstances some injury is common except in the hardiest broad-leaved evergreens and conifers, and some losses may occur among plants near the border line of hardiness. Fortunately, such extreme weather does not occur with great frequency. But it is impossible to foretell the severity of a winter, therefore it is always well to provide protection for young plants whose hardiness is in question.

Enough has been said to indicate that plants are sometimes considered as wanting in hardiness when some peculiarity of their environment or treatment is responsible for such damage as they suffer in winter. Blaming the weather is not always the complete answer for their failure to live up to expectations.

3 Soil Preparation

Anyone who builds or purchases a house, and the planting remains to be done to his pleasure, will conjure up in his mind a picture of how he would like the property to appear when the plants are established, and evergreens in varied assortment will usually play an important part in its composition. The fulfillment of the scheme sometimes proves disappointing because the plants fail to grow as well as anticipated. Assuming suitable plants are selected, any failure is probably due to insufficient soil preparation which, to repeat a timeworn expression, is just as necessary to a garden as a sound foundation to a house. It is no mere figure of speech to say that half the secret of success lies in giving the plants a good start in their new location.

The plants will prove to be no better than the environment provided for them, and the soil in which they must grow is a very important part of that environment. Once they are planted any further soil improvement must be from the surface, and though this is possible to a limited degree at a later period, it is most important that they first be given the opportunity to become established under the most favorable conditions. Nonetheless, it is not difficult to appreciate the tendency of the inexperienced to think only of the appropriateness to its surroundings of that portion of a plant visible above ground, and to forget the need for the unseen portion, the roots, to be equally suitably situated. Unless the roots are in a medium that encourages their multiplication the visible portion of the plant will become unsatisfactory no matter how well placed it may be from a decorative viewpoint.

Soils vary greatly in quality and composition, and before the owner assumes the soil of his new garden does not require some improvement it is advisable to seek competent local advice about its character. In level country or gently rolling farm land little more may be required than digging or plowing, for the soil will probably be of good depth and have suffered little by erosion. In hilly regions the topsoil is often thin and poor, and, consequently, more extensive preparation is necessary.

It is important to remember that all trees and shrubs when delivered to the planting site, whether they are evergreen or deciduous, balled and burlapped or with bare roots, have suffered the loss of a part of their root system. Therefore, anything done to encourage the quick multiplication of new roots to replace this loss is insurance against the disappointment of subsequent poor growth. Recently there has occurred an increase in the use of preparations intended to reduce the shock of transplanting and encourage rapid root multiplication. After they are added to water according to the manufacturers' directions, some may be applied as foliage sprays or be poured onto the soil, while others are used only in the latter manner.

Sometimes land drainage is a necessary first step in soil improvement, but only when there is sufficient evidence of the need for it should it be undertaken, as overdraining can be as serious as the lack of it. It is not customary to build houses in swampy ground, and in any building development in a low-lying area the drainage of the whole area should have been undertaken before the houses were built. Where artificial drainage is necessary on a country property in a wet area, a stream or pond may be available into which the drainage water can be led, as such outlets are to be found more frequently in the country than in or near towns. But until a suitable outlet is assured it is useless to think of artificial drainage, regardless of where the property is located, except for extremely small areas within a garden when a "dry" well may be sufficient.

When lines of drainage tiles must be laid near proposed plantings of trees, the joints between the tiles in these locations should be set in cement or they invariably become filled with roots, and then the drains cease to function. Hardpan is present below some soils, and is another cause of wet ground. When this impervious layer is near the surface it is sometimes possible to break it up with a subsoil plow, but when it is below the reach of a plow and its formation is such that water is held near the surface, it can be broken by dynamiting, and if this is done by an expert worker it will hardly disturb the surface. Where extensive tree planting is to be undertaken, particularly when the ground is very stony or among rocks, the planting holes are sometimes loosened by dynamiting in order to reduce planting cost which, under these conditions, is very heavy when the work is all done manually.

Badly drained soils are unsuitable for the majority of evergreens, whether their failure to rid themselves of excess water is due to clay or inadequate natural or artificial drainage, and in such circumstances some of the more water-tolerant deciduous trees and shrubs would be more satisfactory.

Unless the borders, or stations for individual plants, have previously been decided upon they can be marked out as soon as any drainage problems are settled. Whatever soil-improving materials are to be used can be spread over these areas and be dug in or, if their size justifies it, be plowed in or worked in with a rotary cultivator. Cow manure and stable manure are the best soil improvers, but stable manure should not be used until it is past the stage of active fermentation. These materials improve both heavy and light soils, the former by increasing aeration and drainage, and in the latter they serve as a binder and as storage for moisture. In addition they provide a slowly available source of plant food and a medium in which roots readily multiply. Unfortunately, manure from stables and cow barns is increasingly difficult to obtain, particularly in or near towns, so it is often necessary to use substitutes.

Compost and partly decayed leaves have the same good physical qualities in the soil as manures, but their nutritive value is lower. Peat moss is an excellent soil conditioner and decays slowly. All kinds of plants flourish in it as well as those requiring a particularly acid soil. It is sometimes possible to obtain locally material known as "humus" that is as satisfactory for general use as peat moss, but as it varies in quality depending upon its source, it should be used only on the recommendation of someone who is familiar with it or after it has been analyzed. Usually it is not acid, and therefore not suitable for the Heath group of plants. Dried animal manures are good but lack the desirable bulk of raw manures and consequently add little to the humus content of the soil. Used alone or, better still, in addition to compost, decayed leaves, or commercial humus, they have considerable value. Fresh poultry manure should be used with extreme caution as it may cause extensive injury to plants. After it is air-dried and passed through a sieve it can be distributed more evenly and, if used in moderate amounts, with less likelihood of deleterious effects. In established gardens a better method is to add the fresh droppings to the compost heap, then they will not only enrich the compost but hasten its decay.

A light application of a complete fertilizer, with or without bulky organic matter, can be used though these preparations are of a temporary nature, and, previous to planting, something of more lasting quality is preferable. As a rule it is better to restrict the use of fertilizers to a later period in the life of a planting, when they may be applied to individual plants or to sections of the planting as may seem advisable. If used indiscriminately, overluxuriant growth may result, and where plants of the Heath family are to be grown they may prove injurious. Organic fertilizers specially prepared for evergreens are now obtainable, though they are intended more specifically for plants of the Heath group.

Lime should be used with caution, and is necessary only if the soil is very acid. It should not be used unless the degree of soil acidity is known or until it has been ascertained by analysis. State experiment stations will make the analysis, and usually give instructions as to how the soil samples are to be taken. Except for plants known to require a definite soil acidity it is unnecessary to worry too much about it, as the majority are tolerant of a rather wide range. Most of the evergreens thrive when it is somewhere between pH 5.0 and pH 6.5, and a number of them when it is around the neutral point, pH 7.0. For the Heath plants acidity is important, and for most of them a range of pH 4.5 to pH 5.5 is desirable. For the latter plants hydrated lime or ground limestone, the forms of lime commonly used in gardens, can be most injurious. They do, however, need calcium in very small amounts, and if it is necessary to add it to the soil it may be given as superphosphate, gypsum, or dolomitic limestone.

Very sandy soils lose water rapidly and do not contain enough organic matter to sustain good growth, and they are improved by working into them liberal amounts of the bulky organic materials previously suggested. These increase their water-holding capacity and provide nutrients, and the extensive use of mulches to conserve soil moisture is also advisable. Warm air quickly penetrates these light soils in spring and tends to induce early growth, but lack of sufficient moisture in summer results in a shortened period of growth activity except in a wet season. Unless the plants are given adequate supplies of water as well as manures or fertilizers, the total amount of annual growth is often poor, except in some plants adapted to these conditions.

Loam soils vary from sandy loams at one end of the scale to clay loams at the other, and somewhere between these extremes, other things being equal, are the soils that are not too dry in summer or too wet in winter, so they may be expected to provide a suitable growing medium for a wide range of evergreens.

Heavy clay soils are the most difficult to cultivate, and limit the variety of plants that may be grown. Neither air nor water moves freely in them, and they are cold late into the spring and growth is retarded. Often they remain too wet in late summer and plants continue to grow when they should be ripening, and they are invariably too wet in winter. During extended periods of summer drought they become so hard that when rain comes they absorb it slowly. Almost any coarse, farm, or garden organic wastes added in quantity will aid in conditioning them. Small, leached cinders are sometimes used in addition, and though opinions differ on their merit they are of value if not used to excess. Fine coal ashes should be avoided.

One may question whether many home sites, except on farms, are chosen because of a particular kind of soil. Far more often other considerations, such as the desirability of the location or nearness to place of business or schools, take precedence over any consideration of the soil, and then the best must be made of what is there. But there are so many instances where ingenuity has turned the most unpromising surroundings into places of beauty that it is only logical to believe any soil can be made into a garden if the owner has the desire and persistence.

In many gardens the principal plantings of evergreens are around the foundations of the house, but before any planting is done near a newly built house, some precautions are advisable. When building is completed, the finished surface grade around the house almost invariably differs from the original grade, and is either above or below the latter. Most frequently this is due to the need for excavating for the cellar and foundation walls. During the process of excavation the topsoil, the best part of any soil, in the immediate vicinity of the house may be overlaid with subsoil or, if the grade is lowered, most of it may be carted away. When the new grade is established the covering of topsoil is often negligible or it may contain too much subsoil, and either condition is far from satisfactory for the growth of evergreens. And, in all probability, odds and ends of builders' waste—cement, metal, wood, and brick ends—have been buried near the foundation walls before the soil is returned to them.

When the area of the beds around the house has been marked out, it should be dug over and any rubbish removed. If it is then plain that the upper eight or nine inches is principally subsoil, usually indicated by its light color, a heavy dressing of old manure, peat moss, compost, or leaf mold will aid in its improvement, or enough good topsoil can be brought in to replace all or the greater part of it. But it is better to avoid the latter alternative unless one is sure of obtaining topsoil as, unfortunately, there are too many instances where subsoil no better than that it is to replace has been passed off as topsoil.

Sometimes the original topsoil within the area of the proposed beds is buried comparatively shallowly, up to ten or twelve inches, and digging a few trial holes will show whether this is so. If the trial holes confirm this, double digging will put the topsoil

35

where it properly belongs, back on top. In order to double dig a piece of ground a trench, two feet wide and eighteen to twenty inches deep, is opened across one end of the piece. The overlying subsoil is taken out from this two-foot strip and placed in one heap, and the lower buried topsoil in another. After the first trench is opened, a second strip two feet wide next to the open trench is marked off and its upper layer of overlying subsoil turned into the open trench. Then the lower layer of buried topsoil is thrown up onto it. The original trench is now filled and replaced by the second one, which in turn is filled by reversing the positions of the layers from the third strip. This maneuver is repeated until the end of the bed is reached, and the final trench is then filled with the two layers of soil taken from the first trench.

To become involved in any of this additional work may seem unnecessary to anyone with little experience with the behavior of plants, but it is better to do the work properly at the beginning than to watch plants which were hopefully set out make little growth or actually deteriorate. It is much wiser, and in the end usually cheaper, to correct an unsuitable soil before any planting is done, as it may well save the cost of plant replacements.

An even more disturbing possibility awaits the owner who learns that the whole of the area on which his house and garden stand, along with those of many of his neighbors, has been completely regraded in one major operation. Nowadays this is not an uncommon happening, for thanks to the modern bulldozer the face of an area of land may be changed beyond recognition in a few days.

Apart from the annoyance of the irregular settling of the regraded ground, there is the more serious consideration of its change in quality. Before grading takes place the topsoil is pushed into heaps, later to be spread over the regraded subsoil. But it loses something in the process, its quality is changed. Often an insufficient amount of topsoil is taken off or, due to irregularities in the original surface, too much subsoil is mixed with it. Under these circumstances it is essential to use extra care in preparing all planting areas, and for this purpose bulky organic soil-improving materials are the only satisfactory kind. It may be advisable to undertake soil preparation and planting piecemeal, rather than attempting to do all the work at one time, because of the added cost of making the soil a suitable medium for root growth. This slower method is better than to plant extensively without first amending the soil, and wait vainly for the growth and improvement in the plants that do not materialize.

Several references have been made to the Heath family of plants, the *Ericaceae*, and to some of its likes and dislikes, so a further word about it is called for. The family includes some of the most beautiful flowering broad-leaved evergreens, embracing such familiar examples as Rhododendron, Azalea, Pieris, and Mountain Laurel in addition to many others which, though not so well known or perhaps not so striking in appearance, are almost equally beautiful subjects. They can, however, be disappointing unless the soil meets their requirements. An acid soil is necessary, but acidity alone is not enough.

Few of the really ornamental Heath plants will tolerate water standing about their roots; therefore the soil must allow any excess to pass into a natural or artificial drainage system with reasonable facility. At the same time it must be sufficiently retentive of moisture to permit their fine, hair-like roots to travel freely in it without imminent danger of being killed during periods of dry weather. An ample supply of acid organic material is the best insurance against this kind of injury. The feeding roots of these plants are not far below the surface of the ground, a pretty good indication that air is essential to them, and this explains why they do not succeed in a wet or heavy soil and also why surface cultivation is injurious, as it destroys those roots close to the surface.

However, any free-draining soil that is not alkaline can generally be adapted to their needs with very little extra preparation. Peat moss is the material in most common use in preparing beds or stations for these plants, but oak leaves so far decayed that their original outlines are no longer distinguishable, decayed conifer leaves from beneath old stands of these trees, rotted hardwood sawdust, or tanbark may be used separately or in mixture in the proportion of one third to one half the amount of peat moss. Occasionally peat moss is entirely omitted and these other materials used separately or in mixture with equally good results. Old cow manure is excellent for them, and may be used with benefit when preparing the beds. Other safe organic manures include cottonseed and soybean meals and tankage. Among the inorganic fertilizers only those which are acid should be used. In addition to the nutritive value of the latter, they are generally necessary to offset the loss of nitrogen which is taken from the soil by some substances employed as mulches, and also aid in the decomposition of these mulches. Sawdust, leaves from trees other than oak or conifers, compost, and the variable material known as humus are some of those which come within this category. Sulfate and nitrate of ammonia serve this purpose, but nitrate of soda should not be used.

On the lighter soils a layer of peat moss or a mixture as suggested above can be spread on the surface of the bed to a depth of three or four inches and be forked in. On the heavier soils it is necessary to use greater amounts of these materials and to add coarse sand. Some of the Heath plants, notably Rhododendrons and Azaleas, are so highly regarded that attempts are frequently made to grow them in alkaline soils, but unless the would-be grower realizes the difficulties he is up against they are often very disappointing. Even though the soil is made acid before planting, soil water from the surrounding area seeps in and again changes the soil reaction to alkaline. When beds are prepared in this kind of soil it should be removed to a depth of eighteen inches and replaced with one that is naturally acid, and to which peat moss or other organic ingredients have been added. To prevent capillary water rising from the soil below the bed, a layer of small stones or gravel is advisable. The surface of the finished bed should be three or four inches above the surrounding grade so that surface water will not run over it. Sometimes the bed is entirely filled with organic materials, but most of these plants make more satisfactory growth when there is some mineral admixture in the soil.

When the foliage of Heath plants in such beds in alkaline areas begins to turn yellow, it is good evidence the soil is becoming less acid. Testing it regularly, two or three times during the season, will indicate when a change is taking place, and measures may be taken to correct it. Several materials are employed for this purpose, but they need to be carefully used. Quite recently a new agent has proved very effective, and is likely to find extensive use in the future. This is chelated iron, a highly concentrated but readily soluble form of iron that may be spread on the soil as a powder or used as a foliage spray after it is dissolved in water. It is sold under several trade names, and the manufacturers' instructions should be closely followed.

Finely powdered sulfur is another of these substances, and the amount to use will vary with the nearness to alkalinity of the soil. One to two pounds per 100 square feet is the usual application, but unless the soil pH is known the smaller amount should be used. Sulfur does not quickly bring about a change to green foliage, so several weeks should be allowed to elapse before making a second application. Another material with the same use is aluminum sulfate, and though it is quicker in producing results, its use is rather more hazardous as a heavy concentration of aluminum in the soil is liable to kill the plants. Three or four pounds per 100 square feet may be used as a trial. Of these two materials, the wiser choice in most cases would be to depend upon the slower but safer action of sulfur.

Iron sulfate and magnesium sulfate are also used to change yellowing foliage back to green, and either may be applied as a foliage spray at the rate of one ounce per gallon of water, or to the soil at a trial rate of two pounds per 100 square feet, to be repeated after three or four weeks if the first application does not give the desired result.

Another cause of soil alkalinity may be the domestic water supply used to supplement rainfall. Water from a public source is usually alkaline, and when artificial watering must be frequently resorted to, in time it may cause a change undesirably near the alkaline point.

When plants of the Heath family are grown in soils not ideally suited to them some of these aids to their cultivation will be necessary quite frequently, and because of the difference in pH of some of the materials used for mulching, and of the water supply other than rainfall, they are sometimes necessary in soils much more nearly approaching their needs.

However, there are many instances where Heath plants are grown with considerable success in prepared beds in alkaline regions, but in these cases there is nothing haphazard about their management. It is only through constant attention to details and by experimenting with a variety of treatments that it is possible to learn which are the most suitable for a particular set of conditions.

4 Planting and Aftercare

Plans for landscaping a garden should be made before the ground is prepared in order to determine which parts are to be occupied by lawns and service area in addition to the tree and shrub plantings. In larger gardens, where one or several features will be added, such as tennis court, swimming pool, perennial, rose, or vegetable garden, these must be located before planting begins.

The actual planting may be supervised by the landscape architect who prepared the plan, or by a nursery firm supplying both plan and plants. A homeowner who decides to do his own planning and supervision, but has only a general knowledge of plant material and planting methods, should learn as much as possible of the rate of growth and average mature size of the plants he proposes to use so that they may be spaced accordingly. Young, comparatively small plants often give little indication of their rate of growth, and the commonest fault is to

41

overcrowd them, but neither should they be set so far apart as to appear lost in the planted area. Also, some plants usually prove more suitable than others to the climate, soil, or location, so that a few years later some moving or rearrangement will be desirable.

As a general rule, groups of one kind of shrub, three or more plants of the same kind, are more effective in the landscape than a great mixture of single examples, though single large specimens can be used to provide points of difference and interest among the groups.

Sometimes, however, some other arrangement of the planting is necessary, as when it is the intention of the owner to combine shrubs, herbaceous perennials, and other summer-flowering plants in a common border. In this event there may be a solid planting of shrubs with the more temporary occupants in front of them, or the latter may be used as temporary fillers among the shrubs, to be removed as the shrubs require the space. In either of these instances perennials which spread rapidly by means of underground stems should be avoided, as they are often extremely difficult to eradicate if they become established among the roots of the shrubs.

After the system of planting is decided, the next consideration is of the most suitable period of the year to undertake it, and how the plants are to be handled in order to make reasonably certain they will be quickly re-established in their new quarters. Though the homeowner may have no intention of supervising or undertaking the planting, it is desirable that he know something of the way in which plants are taken up in the nursery, how they should be treated after they are delivered to the garden, how they should be planted, and, when they are again safely in the ground, how they are to be cared for.

Planting is usually undertaken at times when plants are not in active growth or while the new growth is still soft and immature. There are two periods of the year when this is possible, either after growth ceases in the fall, or before or just as it begins in spring. The fall period covers the latter half of August, all September, and occasionally October in the milder areas, but for the greatest welfare of the plants it is better to do the work in the earlier part of this period. In early fall the year's growth is finished and is maturing, the intense heat of summer is past, the nights are longer and cooler, but there is still enough warmth in the soil to induce the growth of new roots.

The spring planting season begins as soon as the ground is dry enough to be in nicely workable condition, and continues until shortly after new growth in evergreens is evident; and for the northeastern section mid-April to mid-June covers this requirement, but further south it begins proportionately earlier.

Which of these two periods is the more suitable to a region will depend upon local climatic conditions, for if the winter is severe following fall planting serious injury or loss may result, as the plants have not enough time to become properly re-established even though they make some new roots before winter puts a stop to this activity. Plants set out in spring have a full growing season ahead of them, and if they receive the necessary attention as to watering during the summer they are better equipped to face their first winter in new quarters. Within recent years foliage sprays that are designed to reduce the loss of water by transpiration have become available. By their use the planting period is lengthened at both ends of the season until it is becoming an almost continuous summer activity. When applied on the approach of winter these same sprays give a measure of protection during that season.

Broadly speaking, fall planting is usually safe along the coastal area north of New York City, and in most areas south of it, but spring is to be preferred in the colder northern inland regions. However, elevation above sea level, the nature of the soil, and any peculiar local climatic conditions should all be considered before deciding in favor of fall planting.

Evergreen trees and shrubs intended for landscaping purposes are dug up in the nursery with the roots enclosed in a ball of soil which is immediately wrapped in burlap and tightly tied before the plant is taken out of the hole. The purpose of the burlap is to prevent the ball of soil from disintegrating, and to

Left, evergreen balled. *Right,* ball wrapped in burlap.

keep it so firm that the roots do not become detached from the soil. This operation is called balling and burlapping and in nursery catalogues is abbreviated to the letters B & B, which follow the names of evergreen and of some deciduous plants.

In order that the ball of soil shall be no greater in size than is necessary to contain sufficient roots to provide the plant with an adequate supply of soil water after it is planted, it is made as small as the nurseryman's experience has shown is safe, depending upon the kind and size of plant. Also, if the ball is made too large the roots are unable to do their share in holding the soil together and it is then liable to break apart of its own weight.

In the better nurseries periodic transplanting or root-pruning is practiced to induce a compact mass of roots to develop near the base of the plants. Nevertheless, in order to obtain the smallest practicable ball some roots must be sacrificed in the digging, and a large proportion of those sacrificed are the younger ones which bear the root hairs through which water is absorbed. Following this loss, it is essential that those roots within the burlap suffer no further handicap, and if the soil is loose within this cover instead of quite solid, then the roots are no longer attached to it. When this happens there is every probability the plant will not survive after it is planted, and any evergreen with the burlap full of loose soil should be rejected, for its chance of survival is no better than if it had been dug with bare roots. If it were possible to transplant evergreens with bare roots in the manner in which many deciduous trees and shrubs are handled, the added cost of balling and burlapping would not be justified. To reduce the possibility of soil ball breakage, balled plants should be handled as little as possible, and then very carefully.

Balled and burlapped evergreens should not be allowed to

stand exposed to sun and wind for any extended period. If they cannot be planted within a short time after they are delivered to the planting site, they should be placed close together under trees or on the north side of a building, with extra burlap, hay, or other protective material laid around and over the balls, and be kept moist.

Except for quite small plants, the holes in which they are to be planted should be at least eighteen inches greater in diameter than that of the soil ball. This space allows sufficient room around the ball to make the backfill firm with the aid of a tamper or the heel of the planter's shoe, with little danger of breaking the ball, which may happen if a smaller space is allowed in which to work. As the holes are dug the topsoil should be placed on one side and the subsoil on the other, and when backfilling, the topsoil is placed in contact with the ball and the subsoil around the outer edge.

The holes should be dug rather deeper than the estimated required depth, with the sides perpendicular and not sloping toward the center. To compensate for the extra soil removed from the bottom of the hole, a similar amount of topsoil, old manure, compost, humus, peat moss, or any decayed organic matter is forked into the bottom and then tramped down to prevent undue settling. This improves the soil beneath the plant and provides a better medium for the deeper roots. Then final adjustments are made to the depth of the hole. The soil mark on the stem of the plant indicates the depth at which it was planted in the nursery, and the necessary depth of the hole can be gauged by holding a stick upright against the ball and measuring the distance from this soil mark to the ground.

Here it may be noted that it is poor policy to attempt to remove the burlap covering the soil ball either before or after the plant is placed in the hole, for if it is removed there is considerable risk of the ball breaking apart during the backfilling and tamping. Burlap quickly rots in the soil and offers no effective resistance to the emission of roots.

After adding or removing soil from the hole to a depth equal to that measured with the stick against the soil ball, place the plant in it and lay a straight board across the hole at normal ground level and close to the stem of the plant. Small corrections for depth of planting can then be made by raising or lowering

Measuring depth of plant ball

the soil ball according to whether the soil mark on the plant stem is above or below the board. In either event this may be done by laying the plant over on one side and removing or adding a little soil. It is then laid over on the opposite side and the process repeated, and when the plant is again set in an upright position the ball should be at the correct depth. If it is necessary to lift the plant out of the hole it will indicate that the preparatory work has been carelessly done.

Though many more plants are killed by being planted too deeply rather than too near the surface, with most of them the soil mark on the stem may safely be an inch or so below the finished grade. But subjects which root very near the surface, those of the Heath group, for example, should never be planted deeper than they were previously.

Young trees with a single trunk and shrubs with upright stems must again be erect in their new locations, and any deviation from this position can be corrected by easing up the ball on the side that falls from the perpendicular and tamping a little soil under it. Viewing a plant from two positions at right angles to one another will show when it is upright.

The hole is now ready for backfilling, and soil is thrown into the space around the ball in layers four or five inches deep. Each layer is roughly leveled, then made firm with a tamper or the heel of the shoe. In heavy or wet soils tamping should not be carried to such an extreme that the soil is puddled and made impervious to air, and because of this possibility planting should be delayed when the soil is very wet. The purpose of tamping is to hold the plant in position and to compact the soil just sufficiently so that there are no unfilled air pockets. When the hole is filled to the shoulder of the ball, that part of the burlap still exposed is cut off or loosened from around the stem and laid back on the tamped soil, after which the plant may be watered in and the remainder of the hole filled but not tamped.

Sometimes the backfill is washed in with water from a hose instead of being tamped. For plants with a large soil ball the space around the ball is half filled with soil, and water is run in until it becomes thin mud. This is necessary to drive the air out of the soil and so avoid air pockets. Water seldom runs evenly through the backfill, and to overcome this a spade or stick should be used to stir it, particularly near the ball, to allow the soil to be more readily saturated. The remainder of the hole is then filled to within a few inches of the surface, and the process repeated. After the excess water has had time to drain away planting is completed. Trees and shrubs planted in this manner are as firm in the ground after the backfill has dried out to the condition of the surrounding soil as when the backfill is tamped.

When stations for single plants are to be dug in a lawn the work should be cleanly done so that when it is finished the lawn shows no evidence of recent planting operations. To ensure this, burlap is laid on the grass, and onto this the soil from the planting hole is thrown. The turf is taken up and placed on one side, and as the hole is dug topsoil and subsoil are kept separate. When the hole has been dug rather deeper than required, and the bottom dug over, the·turf is thrown into it, grass side down, and chopped up into small pieces with the spade. Any soil-improving materials are mixed with the soil before backfilling. As the soil under a lawn is usually quite compact and, therefore, not in the best condition for the spread of tree or shrub roots, planting holes should be of ample size—eighteen to twenty-four inches greater in diameter than the width of the ball for small plants, and three feet or more for large ones.

It is not usually necessary to prune the branches of evergreens when they are transplanted, though this is the proper practice with deciduous trees and shrubs with bare roots where it is required to balance the amount of roots they lose when taken up in the nursery. But as already explained, balled and burlapped evergreens should contain a sufficient quantity of roots in the soil balls to supply them with the water they require until new roots begin to grow, which should eliminate any need for branch pruning.

The homeowner who proposes to move evergreens from one position to another in his garden may be helped by a brief description of how a ball of earth is dug with a plant and then wrapped in burlap. The work must be done carefully or the plants may receive a serious check. If he proposes to do the work without assistance he should realize that the mass of soil on a balled plant does not have to be very large to be too heavy to be handled by one man. Somewhere between fifteen and twenty inches in diameter, depending upon the amount of moisture in the soil, is as large a ball as the average man will be wise to attempt, and then only with the aid of planks on which to pull it out of the old position and slide it into the new one.

First, by running a string around the plant from the base upwards the branches are gathered together into a much smaller spread, but they must not be so tightly drawn in that there is danger of breaking them. Tying up the branches in this manner greatly facilitates balling and replanting. Then with a spade a circle is notched on the ground, with the stem of the plant, or the approximate center of a shrubby one, as its center, and a little beyond the estimated circumference of the ball of earth to be taken up. It is better to err on making the circle too large rather than too small, as the size of the ball is readily made smaller as the work proceeds, but if too small a circle is marked out irreparable damage may be done by cutting off more roots than the plant can properly spare.

Digging begins outside the notched circle and goes down to

such a depth as will leave the mass of fibrous roots within the finished soil ball. This depth will vary from twelve inches for small plants to twenty inches for larger ones, but for the latter it should be a little deeper than the ball to allow for a more efficient working space. If there are not many roots exposed after the circular trench is dug, the mass of soil is made gradually smaller all around with a digging fork until roots are exposed in quantity. A Rhododendron thirty inches tall should have a ball fifteen or sixteen inches in diameter, a size also suitable for a forty-two inch pyramidal conifer. However, if the plant has been standing in the same position for several years it will be wise to increase the size by a few inches, and it is always more important not to destroy roots thoughtlessly than to aim for a particular size of soil ball.

Having decided the diameter of the ball is as small as it is safe to make it, cut off any thick roots projecting from its sides, as the burlap must fit tightly, but small roots may be left. The most critical part of the work comes next, which is cutting away the soil below the ball. It is here that the greatest difficulty will be encountered with roots. The small ones are readily severed with the spade, but the stouter ones will offer resistance, and if efforts to cut them with the spade are persisted in, the jarring may cause the ball to break apart and so ruin the attempt at moving. These stout roots should be located with the hands and cut off close to the ball with pruning shears.

Small plants may have all the basal roots cut immediately and then be gently laid over on one side preparatory to being covered with burlap before they are taken out of the holes. A square of burlap of a suitable size is taken up by one edge with both hands, and with the fingers half its length is gathered into folds. The gathered portion is placed under the edge of the overturned ball, and the plant then laid over in the opposite direction on the half square of burlap that was not gathered. With the plant in this new position it is possible to straighten out the gathered burlap, and when the plant is set upright it should be in its center. The diagonally opposite corners are then knotted on top of the ball. If an overlarge piece of burlap is used the knots will be so big that it will be impossible to make it sufficiently tight to hold the ball safely. Another method is to draw the burlap over the ball and to use two-inch nails as pins to hold it tightly in place. The fibrous roots of Rhododendrons and Azaleas in moderate sizes usually hold the soil so well that tying the burlap to the soil ball may be unnecessary.

For larger plants, usually requiring two men, the work is practically the same except that after the ball is shaped it is not completely severed underneath but allowed to stand on a small earth base or pedestal during the time it is wrapped in burlap. A length of this material is run around the ball until it overlaps a few inches. It need not completely cover the top of the ball but must come well up over its shoulder and be wide enough for its lower edge nearly to meet beneath the plant. For trees with one central stem, a burlap bag or several thicknesses of burlap must be wrapped around the stem close to the ball, and one end of a length of stout cord or rope tied around this cushion. If the cord is tied to the bare stem there is great danger of breaking the bark and doing serious damage to the tree. When there is no single axis but a number of branches arise at or below ground level, as in most shrubs, the cord is passed under the ball close to the pedestal and tied to itself on top of the ball. In either case the running end of the cord is now passed down the side and under the ball close to the pedestal, pulled tight, and again passed round the ball so that when the second cord is at the widest part of the ball it is six or eight inches from the first, and this is repeated until all the burlap is tied in. With a sandy soil or with plants which do not develop a compact mass of fibrous roots, the cords must be closer together than for soils of a heavier texture or plants with a dense root system.

For the larger ball sizes, and where the soil is apt to crumble, it is also necessary to run one or two cords in a horizontal direction, so that the ball is divided into zones of similar width. Such a cord is first tied to one of the vertical cords, passed once around each succeeding vertical cord, and pulled on meanwhile to ensure its tightness, until the circle is completed when it is tied to the vertical cord from which it started. Every cord should now be so tight that it is next to impossible to push a finger under any one of them.

The pedestal and the roots which pass through it into the subsoil are then cut, after which the plant may be laid over on its side. If the pedestal is comparatively small it may be unnecessary to cover the exposed soil with burlap, especially as the plant is to be moved a relatively short distance to its new position. First attempts at balling and burlapping, however, often result in such a large uncovered area at the base that it may be advisable to spread the lower edge of the burlap over it or to use an extra piece which can be held in place by running a few cords across it from the lowest horizontal cord.

Whether evergreens are received from a nursery or moved from one place to another on the property, they should be given water soon after they are planted, that is, unless the backfill was washed in with a hose instead of being tamped. The simplest method is to give water while a few inches of the planting hole remain to be filled, by allowing the water to run slowly into this depression until it is reasonably certain some of it has sunk to the bottom of the backfill. Shortly afterward the remainder of the hole is filled with soil, but these last few inches are not tamped. Another method is to complete the planting and then draw up a rim of soil around the circumference of the original hole and allow the water to run into this saucer-like area. This is the better method of the two as the saucer is already prepared for subsequent waterings during dry weather.

Plants should never be moved when the soil is very dry, as it is often exceedingly difficult to make the soil balls absorb water after they are replanted. For this reason fall planting may be undesirable following a hot, dry summer when the ground is practically devoid of moisture. Though the freshly moved plants may be given water as soon as they are in their new locations, this may not be enough to ensure their re-establishment. It is by no means a rare occurrence, on examining the soil balls of transplants which died during the winter, to find that the cause of their death was this failure to be moistened by artificial watering or the rains and snows of winter. Unless there have been ample rains previous to the time they are to be moved, homeowners who propose to do any transplanting in the fall should take the precaution of thoroughly soaking the ground on which the plants stand a day or two previous to moving them.

When plants are purchased which have been grown in heavy soil, the kind which is most likely to form impervious balls when it is dry, it is sometimes helpful to open the burlap and gently chip the surface of the ball with a trowel or digging fork in order to roughen it and make it somewhat better able to absorb moisture. In dry, sandy soils it is often almost impossible to form a ball that will hold together.

To say that watering should be repeated whenever it is necessary may be correct but is not very enlightening, as its frequency will depend upon the amount of rainfall, the nature of the soil, and the season of the year. It is impossible to be specific about the intervals which should elapse between applications. If the weather is dry, plants set out in the early fall, for example, will require several additional waterings before winter sets in. For those set out later the initial application may well be sufficient if the weather is cool and rainy. An ample supply of water is essential, but air in the soil is as necessary as water, and if the soil is constantly near saturation point those roots injured when the plants were dug may begin to decay instead of putting out new roots. Whether planting is undertaken in autumn or spring, sufficient water must be given during the growing period and early summer, for it is then that they have the greatest need for it, and when there is any question of the rainfall supplying this need artificial watering must not be neglected.

Due to the loss of a portion of its roots when it is taken up for transplanting, those left to a plant have an added task to keep it supplied with enough water until new roots have multiplied in sufficient number to increase the intake. Light rainfalls can be deceptive by creating the impression that because the surface soil is wet it is also wet at greater depths, but such rainfalls do not go deeply enough into the ground to be of any real value to plants, and the upward growth of new roots toward the moister surface is encouraged by such superficial wetting. When the showers cease and a period of hot weather follows, these tender roots will probably be injured or killed. Normal rains or periodic heavy watering induce lateral and downward movement of roots, because the surface soil has an opportunity to dry out to a reasonable degree and discourage the upward growth; consequently plants are in a better position to withstand periods of drought than when the roots are nearer the surface. The same remarks apply to the much favored, but almost useless practice of merely sprinkling newly set out plants with a hose. A sprinkling over the foliage in the evenings of hot days may be of some benefit but is no substitute for thorough, deep watering, which should be done every seven to fourteen days, depending upon the nature of the soil, in dry weather during spring and summer.

Evergreens, and particularly the broad-leaved kinds, are subject to severe injury if their tissues do not contain enough water during the winter. For this reason, both in recent plantings and older established ones, it is advisable to give an ample watering in October and another in November or later if the ground is not frozen, unless there has been an adequate rainfall.

As has been pointed out, the loss of water by transpiration following recent transplanting and the inability of the plant readily to replace it because of its reduced root system are two of the more serious aspects of transplanting evergreens. As a means of reducing this loss, spray materials have been developed which form an almost impervious coating over the foliage. These materials are of plastic or rubber in a solvent and a water carrier, and after the latter have evaporated a thin, but not completely impervious, coating is left on foliage and stems. They are not unsightly, and can be detected only by the slightly glazed or grayish appearance of the leaves. Their use, however, in no way minimizes the need for observing all the precautions necessary for successful transplanting and aftercare. These same materials have value for the winter protection of evergreens in place of the more conventional burlap and other forms of covering mentioned later in this chapter. But for plants known or suspected to be tender, the wiser course is to continue with the more complete coverings, though these sprays are valuable when used on many of the hardier plants.

The need for artificial watering does not necessarily cease when trees and shrubs are established. Periods of drought can occur at any time of year from early spring until the ground freezes the following winter, and it is impossible to estimate their duration, and often they are of purely local occurrence. Depending solely upon rainfall is seldom satisfactory as it varies so much from year to year, and most of the evergreens, but particularly the broad-leaved kinds, require adequate amounts during spring and early summer and again in late fall. However, there are limitations to their need. After shoot and leaf growth for the year are completed, it is desirable that the amount of soil moisture be reduced for a period in order to cause this growth to mature and harden in preparation for winter. Therefore, watering should cease or be drastically cut down during the latter part of summer, approximately the middle of August to the middle of October. When plants have received sufficient amounts by natural or artificial means up to this time, there is no occasion to fear for their welfare during this drying-off period and, so far as rainfall permits, the hardening of evergreens after the year's growth is completed is timely preparation for the trying winter months ahead.

Naturally, there are some exceptions to this as to any other general rule, but in very few years is the rainfall so meager that it should be necessary to give additional water during this time. In the event of an almost complete lack of rainfall, very small plants for example, might suffer injury, as might plants in very sandy soils or those native to wet soils. However, after a dry fall, enough water should be given before the ground freezes so that evergreens do not go into the winter dry at the roots.

Of the several ways in which water may be supplied, permanent installations of galvanized or plastic pipe buried through the center of the border are the most efficient. Sprinkler heads can be attached to these at a suitable height and spaced according to the water pressure. Or short standpipes can be placed at greater distances along the edge of the border but close enough to allow covering the border with a hose.

For small areas and rather low plants some of the lawn sprinklers are satisfactory, though some throw more water around the periphery of the area they are intended to cover than within it, but others have a rectangular spread. Perforated hose is more useful among plants which are set rather close together, such as foundation plantings, than among plants a greater distance apart, as the outflow through the holes is restricted to a rather narrow strip of ground. For the deep watering of individual plants, a water injector is useful. This consists of a hollow, perforated steel pipe, pointed at one end, with a hose attachment at the other. The pointed end is pushed deeply into the ground, and water from a garden hose forced through the perforations into the soil. It can also be used for feeding plants if a fertilizer mixer is attached between faucet and hose.

Whatever method of application is employed, it is better to water thoroughly at rather long intervals than frequently and lightly. Too much water is lost by evaporation in the latter method, and too little sinks sufficiently deeply into the soil to be of real service to roots. Several hours after watering, a few holes can be dug in the area covered by the sprinklers in order to determine how far the water has penetrated, and it should not be less than six inches.

After planting is completed there remains the question of caring for the borders. Weeds will grow between the plants and beneath their branches unless these are very low, and not only for the sake of appearance but because they take a share of plant food and soil moisture, they must be destroyed. Annual control begins early in spring when the borders should be forked over as soon as the surface is reasonably dry, that is, except where Rhododendrons or other members of the Heath family are growing. It is both unnecessary and undesirable to fork deeply—four or five inches is sufficient. In all probability the ground will be overlaid in places with the fallen leaves of deciduous trees from the previous autumn, and these can be turned under unless they have collected in quantity, in which case most of them should be carted away, or possibly they can be distributed evenly and thinly before they are forked in. Weed seeds will have blown in and be present on the surface, but turning over the soil will bury many of them to a depth where the seedlings will be unable to come through the surface. Some weed seeds, however, remain viable in the soil for years until such conditions as depth below the surface, warmth, and moisture are just right for them to germinate and grow, and for some of them these conditions are provided each time the surface is disturbed. As forking proceeds there should be no attempt to leave a smooth surface, though any clods are broken to leave it roughly even. The surface should not be raked, as a loose, rough surface absorbs rainfall more readily than one which is smooth and baked hard by the sun.

If manure or fertilizer is to be used it should be spread before forking begins. Whether there is a need for these materials must depend upon the owner's judgment. Where the borders are properly prepared before any planting is undertaken there may be no occasion to use them for some years, as nothing is gained by forcing luxuriant, soft growth. After the initial spring forking, subsequent weed growth is destroyed by shallow hoeing in dry weather so that the uprooted weeds will die and not be merely transplanted.

Each year the shrubs grow larger and the spaces between them become smaller, and as the roots of most shrubs extend beyond the spread of the branches and may be unnecessarily injured by forking, and also because the canopy of shade cast by most evergreens becomes denser and less favorable for weed growth, eventually the spring forking may be omitted and any weeds which succeed in growing be destroyed with the hoe. Added to which the leaves which fall from the plants begin to form a natural mulch and are a further help in making forking unnecessary.

The ground around any plants of the Heath family should be neither forked nor hoed. A permanent mulch of some of the materials to be mentioned later will prevent the growth of most weeds, and the few which grow in or through it can be pulled out by hand.

In summer, a mulch is a means of conserving soil moisture by preventing its rapid evaporation and at the same time providing a more equable soil temperature. In winter, it is a means of hindering the rate of entry of frost deeply into the ground, thereby allowing evergreens a longer period in which to draw on soil moisture than would be possible without its aid, and, when the ground freezes, to keep it frozen rather than have it subjected to the injurious effects of alternate freezing and thawing. In this way it provides protection for roots.

Mulches may be temporary, as when they are used only in winter for plants not entirely hardy, or for a limited period after planting, in the latter case often the first year. Or they may be made permanent by being renewed periodically, usually once a year. When suitable materials are available in the necessary quantity they are useful for most of the broad-leaved evergreens the year around, and also for doubtfully hardy conifers in winter. For most plants of the Heath family, however, they should be permanent.

Except after spring planting, it is advisable to delay applying mulches until the ground is frozen to a depth of about two inches, or until such time as the frost may be expected to remain in the ground until the end of winter. This is most advisable after fall planting, as there is always the danger of mice tunneling the ground beneath the mulch and feeding on the roots of the plants it was intended to protect. Though there is always this danger it seems to be much greater where the ground has recently been disturbed. Poisoned grain, placed in four-inch drain tiles to keep it out of the reach of birds, is one means of control. The mulch should be kept a few inches away from the plant stems.

There is a variety of materials which may be used for mulching, and some of the more common are: manure, leaves, compost, peat moss, salt hay, straw, excelsior, and cranberry stems. Leaves, and the last four items on this list, are inflammable when dry, and should be used around buildings only after consideration of the damage that may result from a carelessly thrown match or cigarette end, and to ensure greater safety they should be wetted down. Straw, salt hay, and excelsior are so light in color that they may be considered unsuitable in locations where appearance is important.

As a rule, the most generally available mulching material is fallen leaves. Oak leaves are to be preferred, as they do not flatten out so readily as most other kinds, which have a tendency to form layers more or less impervious to water. The principal objection to leaves is the possibility of their being blown away during dry, windy weather. Shrubs with low branches hold them in place, but, otherwise, twiggy branches must be laid on them. A few sticks or stones will anchor salt hay, straw, excelsior, or cranberry stems. Peat moss is satisfactory in winter but in the heat of summer becomes felt-like until thoroughly wet, but mixed with leaf mold it is not open to this objection.

Such materials as manure, compost, leaf mold, or peat moss, which have already undergone partial decay, when used as a temporary mulch after planting, need not be removed but can be allowed to remain and disintegrate. For the sake of appearance it is usually necessary to take up the coarser materials, salt hay, straw, cranberry stems, and excelsior, but also because it is difficult to control the weeds which grow up through them unless the mulch is very thick.

As was previously stated, a permanent mulch should be maintained over the root areas of most plants of the Heath family and is invaluable to them in summer as well as in winter, as they like a cool, moist, root run close to the surface of the ground. The fall of the year is a good time to renew the mulch, as it will then provide extra protection through the winter. In common with other plants requiring winter protection, the fallen leaves from deciduous trees are commonly used because, as a rule, they are most frequently at hand.

It is an old trick to cover the ground under some of these plants, Rhododendrons for example, with as many fallen leaves as the foliage will hide. This is often done, as it is an easy means of getting rid of a surplus of leaves, and then their value as a mulch may become incidental. Where this practice is repeated year after year, they are packed down by snow and rain until a layer of wet, undecayed leaves may eventually form a more or less airtight seal over the surface of the soil, which is detrimental to the plants. A loose covering a foot in depth will generally be ample, unless the surplus is to be removed in spring. Whether too great or too small a quantity is being applied can be judged when the renewal time comes round in the following fall, as the residue from the previous application should be so far decayed that it is little more than finely disintegrated matter. Some gardeners prefer to collect the freshly fallen leaves and store them for a year or two until they are partly decayed, and then use them for mulching.

Oak leaves and Pine needles have an acid reaction as they decay, for which reason they are to be preferred over other kinds of leaves as a mulch for Heath plants. When it is necessary to use the leaves from other trees the soil should be tested periodically to determine whether it is becoming alkaline. If so, a light application of chelated iron, sulfur, magnesium sulfate, or iron sulfate can be used to offset it, or if a fertilizer is also desirable, soybean or cottonseed meal, or tankage, or a small amount of sulfate or nitrate of ammonia can be used. A mulch of peat moss two or three inches in depth should be ample, but it should be thoroughly moistened before it is spread or much of it may blow away or float off during the first heavy rain. Old cow manure is an excellent mulch for these plants.

Devices to protect evergreens from wind and sun during the winter are frequently necessary, and not by any means only through the first winter after planting. In many gardens in exposed situations, public as well as private, they are required for some plants every winter. They vary from the familiar snow fence to more effective completely enclosed structures. A snow fence consists of laths woven together by wires into continuous lengths, with the spaces between laths approximately equal to the width of two laths. A similar fence in common use as shading over young plants in nursery beds has the spaces equal to the width of the laths, and is to be preferred because of this closer spacing. Either of these, when erected on the windward side and some feet away from a planting of evergreens, is sufficient to break the force of the wind to the extent that possible wind injury or "burning" of the plants is considerably reduced. They are held erect by being wired to stakes driven into the ground eight to ten feet apart.

Another screening material is burlap, and though more effective for low plants than a lath fence, it is also more liable to be torn down by high winds just when there is the greatest need for it unless it is carefully erected. Stout stakes must be firmly driven into the ground and the top edge of the roll of burlap tied to a wire strung between the stakes. Much more elaborate

63

than any of these is a solid board fence. It is made up in panels three to five feet high of any convenient length for handling, and the panels erected end to end. The above screens are only intended to give protection from wind, but sun injury is equally serious when plants are frozen, and then another type of shelter is required.

Box-like or tent-like structures serve this purpose, and the shape of the plant will indicate which of them is the more suitable. If the structure is to be flat on top it must be re-enforced with a sufficient number of crosspieces to prevent the top covering tearing away from its fastenings when a mass of frozen snow rests on it, as such an accident may ruin the plant beneath.

Burlap is the usual covering for these shelters, and coarsely woven, open-meshed material is preferable to the heavier, closely woven kind, as it permits a freer passage of air while giving protection from wind and sun and the inside of the shelter does not become so overheated in sunny weather. Green burlap is available, though the color is not very good, but it does not stand out quite so starkly as the natural light brown, but many people still prefer the latter. Laths are sometimes substituted for burlap in order to ensure free passage of air and still provide protection from the sun. The laths are nailed to the framework with a space between laths equal to half the width of a lath, and such structures are less obtrusive if they are painted dark green. Pine or Fir boughs provide excellent protection by breaking the force of the wind and providing shade without preventing the passage of air. These branches may be used in place of burlap or laths and on the same types of framework if additional wooden crosspieces or wires are run along the sides of the structure to which the branches can be tied. To cover single, low plants, the butt ends of the branches are sharpened and pushed into the soil or into holes made with a crowbar, and the outer ends tied together over the plant.

Rather narrow plants, to four or five feet tall, may be completely enclosed in straw or cornstalks. Before the covering is put on, the branches should be drawn together a little with string and a stake driven in by each plant so that wind or a weight of frozen snow will not bend or break it. For low, spreading plants or groups of small plants of a foot or so in height, a covering of evergreen branches, cranberry stems, straw, or salt hay is satisfactory, in addition to or without a mulch on the soil surface depending upon how thickly the tops of the plants cover the ground. Salt hay and straw must not be put on top of the plants as a thick layer or the damp beneath the covering may cause molding, which can do as much harm as exposure to the weather. Cranberry stems and evergreen branches do not hold moisture or pack down as do these other materials. The neatest way to hold any of them in place is to run lines of strings across the bed at right angles to one another, which are tied to short stakes around its edges.

These protective coverings should not be removed on the first mild day in spring, but left until the frost is out of the ground and it is reasonable to suppose the coldest winter winds are a thing of the past. With straw or salt hay it is advisable to take off part of the covering a couple of weeks earlier to allow air to circulate more freely around the plants.

After a heavy snowfall there is often a considerable amount of damage to foundation plantings due to snow sliding off steeply pitched roofs. It is becoming increasingly common to install snow guards above house gutters or between the roof tiles at the time a house is built in order to prevent this kind of accident. Where such precautions have not been taken on a house with a steep roof, it is advisable to build a temporary, stout wooden framework over the plants around the foundation to intercept masses of sliding snow. If neatly made and painted such a structure need not be an eyesore, and even though it adds nothing to the appearance of the house it is preferable to running the risk of having an expensive planting partially or completely ruined.

Another worth-while precaution should be taken against what can be the damaging effect of a heavy snowfall during still, windless weather, as subsequently some evergreens may be badly injured. Unless the snow is very wet it can be quite readily dislodged by gently striking a plant with the flat side of a broom. If the mass of snow is allowed to remain on the plants and a light thaw follows after which the snow freezes to them, it is impossible to knock it off without injuring the plants. And the weight of frozen snow can be so great that the branches are pulled apart, often permanently, or broken in the crotches. This possibility may be partly overcome if at the approach of winter a string is run spirally around each plant liable to have its branches pulled apart, drawing it a little tighter than the plant's normal spread.

Evergreen hedges can be protected by running chicken wire along each side, in close contact with the hedge, and tying the netting to stakes long enough to support the upper edge of the netting against the upper edge of the hedge. As an added pre-caution against the hedge spreading under a weight of snow, strands of wire are run across the hedge a few feet apart and fastened to the upper edge of each line of chicken wire. Some-times a single strand of wire, or two strands twelve to eighteen inches apart for taller hedges, is used in place of netting, but does not give an equal amount of safety. But having provided any of these safeguards, it is always good policy to use a broom to dislodge as much snow as possible as soon as it ceases falling.

Staking or guying of newly planted trees is usually necessary. Simply because evergreen trees are planted with a ball of earth is no guarantee they will not be blown off the perpendicular by strong winds. This can happen at any time of the year, but probably the period of greatest danger is early fall, when it is not uncommon for gale winds to follow in the wake of torrential rains. The ground is then so soft that a tree must be very firmly rooted if it is to remain standing upright.

The extent to which trees are exposed to the wind will determine the smallest sizes requiring support, but it is much simpler to do the work immediately after planting than to set a tree upright and install it after the damage is done, as often a great deal of digging is necessary to bring a tree again to an upright position. Supports should be maintained for two or three years, depending upon the size of the tree.

Three guy wires should be used for trees ten or more feet in height and one end of each wire run through a short length of old hose and these in turn looped around the trunk above a branch at about two thirds of the tree's height. The loops must be sufficiently large to prevent constriction of the trunk prior to the time the guy wires are no longer needed and are removed. The lower ends of the wires may be twisted around stakes driven into the ground in the form of an equilateral triangle about the tree's base beyond the spread of the branches. For tall trees it is better to bury eighteen-inch, stout stakes horizontally a similar distance below ground as anchors, and it is then impossible for them to be pulled out of the ground. The objectionable feature of guy wires is the danger of tripping over or running into them, as they are not readily seen. Sometimes small pieces of cloth are tied to them to call attention to their presence, but a neater method is to tie a four- or five-foot, thin bamboo cane lengthwise to each wire. The canes are soon discolored and not then obvious at a distance.

A single, vertical stake is most frequently used for supporting smaller trees, but there is great danger of the trunk being injured by rubbing against the top of the stake unless care is taken to tie tree to stake in such a manner that this cannot happen. In positions where appearance is not a first consideration, the stake can be driven at an angle to the tree so that it crosses the trunk, and if it projects a few inches beyond the trunk there is little danger of chafing.

Whatever the method of support, stake and tree are held together either by a wire run through a short piece of hose looped around the trunk or with cord. With the latter, a strip of burlap is wrapped around the trunk to form a cushion between tree and stake and thus prevent the cord cutting into the bark. Ties should be examined once a year to see that they are holding and are not causing constriction. When cord is used for the ties, it should be renewed every year, for if left longer it may decay and allow the trunk to be injured by rubbing against the top of the stake.

5 Pruning

Pruning is the cutting away or shortening of parts of a plant, usually shoots or branches, but in view of the many examples of ruthless, needless cutting that pass for pruning, it seems appropriate to suggest that before any pruning is undertaken there be a definite reason for it. The results of thoughtless cutting may require years to repair, if repair is possible. The principal reason for pruning evergreens, broad-leaved or conifers, is the hope of producing a more beautiful plant, whether applied to its shape or its flowering, but its cultural requirements are more often the primary means to this end.

When any kind of evergreen has been growing for a long enough period in one position so that it may be assumed it has had time to become established, poor performance, as may be indicated by insufficient shoot and leaf growth, poor foliage color, or a number of dead or dying stems or branches, is evidence something is wrong with its treatment or environment. It may not be receiving a sufficient amount of sunlight or it may be overexposed. The soil moisture may be inadequate or excessive, or the fault may lie with the soil itself. In or near cities the plant may be literally smothering under the coating of soot and dirt covering its foliage and stems. Or insects so small they are not readily detected, red spider mites and some scale insects, for example, may be sapping its vitality.

Given such conditions, no amount of pruning will be of any use toward producing a better plant until the cause of its unsatisfactory behavior is corrected. Pruning is not a cure-all, though it can increase or check vigor of growth under suitable conditions, and is of little service to a plant making poor growth because it is in the wrong environment or is lacking the cultural care necessary to keep it healthy.

It is also important to realize that beauty in a plant does not necessarily mean extreme regularity of outline. Each kind of evergreen when suitably placed can be expected to assume a characteristic shape, and if pruning is needed it should aim to enhance this feature, but unfortunately it often destroys it.

A common reason for excessive pruning is the improper placement of shrubs. So far as may be judged, those should be chosen which are appropriate in size for the positions they are to occupy. It is a mistake to plant a shrub of vigorous habit in a position adequate only for one of moderate growth, and to attempt to keep it to the proportions suitable to the position by constant pruning. While some plants are much more tolerant than others of repeated close cutting, the usual end result of such severe restriction is either a plant with little character and very artificial appearance, or one completely ruined.

There are exceptions to this as to any other generalization, some of which are dealt with later, but one may be mentioned here. A common reason for pruning is to increase density of branching, particularly in shrubs which have a more open habit of growth than is generally desirable in ornamentals. This can often be accomplished, without materially altering the natural shape of the plant, by cutting off most of the terminal growth of the previous year on the strongest shoots. The early years in the life of a shrub are the important ones for this kind of pruning, and if necessary it may be repeated annually, depending upon the rate of growth, until the required density is obtained.

The majority of evergreen shrubs do not require so much pruning in order to develop their best features as is needed by many deciduous flowering shrubs. Both the broad-leaved and coniferous kinds in common use naturally form plants sufficiently dense, with little or no aid in the way of pruning, though by no means are they always regular in outline. When received from the nursery they should have been pruned often enough in the formative stages to be amply supplied with shoots and branches, and subsequent natural multiplication of these parts may make further pruning unnecessary. But under the best conditions there are always some plants which do not behave in the way they are expected to, so there need be no hesitation about shortening some branches in order to increase density of habit if it is obviously desirable and will not destroy the plant's ultimate form. Occasionally one branch is stronger and becomes more prominent then its fellows and if not checked will give the plant a lopsided appearance. Such offenders may be cut back to just within the body of the plant immediately above the point where a fork is formed by a smaller side shoot.

Pruning shears, a small pruning saw, a heavy pruning knife, and possibly hedge shears are the minimum requirements in the way of tools, but in addition a full-sized pruning saw and either a combined pole pruner and pole saw, or one of each, are necessary for gardens containing many trees.

When shrubs are pruned, the pruning wounds as a rule are

not very large and they should not be in young trees except following wind breakage or other accidents. Though it is true that any break in the bark of a tree or shrub may serve as a point of entry for decay organisms, actually this danger is not very great so far as it concerns small wounds in healthy plants. But in order to be on the safe side it is as well to protect the cut ends of branches over a half inch in diameter with tree-wound paint.

When a large branch in either a tree or a shrub is to be shortened, it should be cut back to an actively growing side shoot in order to avoid leaving a stub, that is, a small or large length of branch devoid of shoot growth. Stubs eventually die back and are always a potential source of decay to the trunk or branch from which they arise. When a branch is to be completely removed, it should be cut off flush with that part of the tree or shrub from which it originates and not an inch or several inches beyond the point of union, or a stub is left.

Cuts made with a saw in any kind of plant should be immediately smoothed over with a pruning knife, as a smooth surface heals more quickly and decay organisms are less likely to establish themselves than on a rough one.

Evergreen hedges and evergreens used for accent purposes in formal gardens and similar positions are usually pruned with hedge shears, as the work can be done more satisfactorily and quickly than with pruning shears. With these exceptions and a few to be mentioned later, frequent shearing is objectionable because the sheared plants appear altogether too artificial, too much as though they had been cast in molds, and the practice of regularly shearing all kinds of conifers in a garden cannot be too strongly condemned. It not only makes the plants look ridiculous, but the garden as a whole takes on the appearance of a freak show. Nevertheless, there are formal gardens where the plants are sheared into pyramids, columns, globes, and similar shapes, and if the plants used are those which by their natural habit lend themselves to this kind of treatment and the work is skillfully done, the result is often quite effective. The extreme in this type of work is topiary, where the plants are pruned and trained into the figures of men, animals, birds, and other forms, which has been the target for ridicule as being altogether too unnatural, as indeed it is. But it at least has the merit of requiring considerable forethought, skill, and patience for its successful accomplishment. For the atrocious mound-shaped objects into which all kinds of conifers are often sheared, strong arms and a lack of imagination are the only requisites. There is little object in planting a variety of kinds if a few stiffly formal shapes are all that is required, for the beauty of the plants lies in their different habits of growth, contrasting or harmonizing with others in their near vicinity, as well as in their shades of color.

Where formality of appearance is not the first consideration but restriction of growth is desirable, it will take longer to go over a plant with pruning shears and cut back the stronger shoots, but as the weaker ones are not cut the plant is left with a softer, more pleasing outline than when it is "barbered" with hedge shears.

The greatest need for pruning evergreens occurs, as a rule, in foundation plantings, where it is customary, in order to obtain an immediately pleasing effect, to set the plants closer together than would be the case in a border, and consequently they will probably fill the space available to them in a shorter time. However, if plants of comparatively slow growth are selected and they are not greatly overcrowded when planted, a little judicious pruning, the shortening or removal of a branch here and there should keep the planting attractive for many years.

Very hard pruning into old wood is seldom advisable for evergreens, no matter what their location in the garden. Few of the conifers will tolerate it but will die as a result, and, if they live, recovery is exceedingly slow and they are likely to assume peculiar shapes as they recover. The Yews, *Taxus*, are one of the exceptions, as they may be severely pruned and survive, but only when they have been badly neglected is such hard usage justified.

Sometimes old Rhododendrons are thin in growth or outgrow their positions, and the question arises of the advisability of heavy pruning in order to secure more compact plants. There is always some risk of loss following this treatment, and the more severe the pruning the greater the possibility of their failure to make new shoots from the old, cut-back stems. It must not be overlooked that sparse growth may be due to other causes than the normal growth habit of the plants, though some horticultural varieties of Rhododendron are more prone to it than others. It may be due to impoverishment of the soil, hence the value of feeding and of a permanent mulch over the root area. Or they may be growing in a soil normally too dry for them, and are not watered artificially or in sufficient amounts. Under such conditions pruning will be of little eventual benefit unless the cause is corrected. When it is decided there is no alternative to hard pruning, the work should be done in spring, but the plants will be unsightly for a few years afterwards.

Occasionally younger Rhododendrons show too many leggy stems, and then a less drastic form of pruning may be practiced. In spring, or from late summer onward, it is usually a simple matter to distinguish flower buds from growth buds, as flower buds are broad and fat and by comparison growth buds are thin. If a flower bud has not developed and the shoot is terminated by a growth bud, this may be broken off just above the leaves before growth commences, and shoots should begin to grow from some of the small buds in the leaf axils. It is from the latter type of bud that new shoots grow when the terminal bud is a flower bud. In the absence of a flower bud some horticultural varieties of Rhododendron have a tendency to develop only one or two terminal growth buds, though this is also induced by poor culture and is the reason for sparse growth.

This bud removal, however, is not always sufficient for the purpose in view, a denser plant, in which case, either before growth begins or immediately after flowering, that part of the shoots which grew in the previous year, or it can be a little more drastic and include also those portions which are two years old, may be cut off just above the next lower cluster of leaves. Shoots will not be produced from the naked portion of stem between two sets of leaves. It is no less important that the plants be fertilized, adequately watered, and mulched in the succeeding year.

For Rhododendrons, Andromedas or Pieris, Mountain Laurel, and for the larger flowered Azaleas another practice is recommended—a form of pruning, though not generally referred to by that name. This is removing the seed vessels as soon as flowering is finished, for they have no decorative value when they mature. It is very easily done by taking the stem of the spent flower cluster between thumb and first finger and bending it over until it breaks off at its base above the leaves. Removing the seed vessels allows the plant to use its energy to promote increased shoot growth instead of devoting it to developing the seeds. This practice is not enough in itself to ensure equal or greater production of flowers in the following year, as other factors also are responsible for flower-bud formation, but it will increase the probability of their production and result in stronger shoot growth.

Among coniferous shrubs some require more pruning than others. To be counted in this group are some of the varieties of the Sawara False-cypress, *Chamaecyparis pisifera,* when used in foundation plantings, for which purpose they are usually much too vigorous, as they soon begin to cover windows and doorways unless kept in check. The greatest offenders in this respect are var. *plumosa,* and its colored forms *plumosa aurea* and *plumosa sulphurea,* and var. *squarrosa.* The var. *plumosa* is a very attractive plant in sizes six-to-ten-feet tall or taller, if it is closely pruned or sheared just before growth begins each year. When it is planted in a border and not pruned it sometimes becomes thin in habit and too much old dead foliage is evident.

Chamaecyparis pisifera var. *squarrosa* is familiar for its filmy, blue-gray foliage, but when allowed to grow at will is apt to assume a rather floppy, untidy shape in its early years. Any of the above varieties are improved if they are closely pruned in spring, or sheared if they are in foundation plantings. Var. *filifera,* and its colored form *filifera aurea,* though not so rampant as the foregoing, should be given a little attention at the same time, but for them pruning to prevent some branches being over-developed, often near the base of the plant, is usually sufficient.

Swiss Mountain Pine, *Pinus Mugo* var. *Mughus,* is a well-merited favorite for foundation and bank plantings, but individual plants vary considerably in rate of growth. They should be low and broad and then may need little or no pruning, but others equally attractive in appearance while they are small assume a much more rapid upward growth once they are established in a new position, and if this is a foundation planting pruning will probably be necessary to keep them low. This may be done in the so-called "candle" stage, that is, when the new spring shoots have made their growth in length and are still very soft, but before the leaves expand. In this condition, the "candles" may be pinched back half their length, and buds will form in some of the rudimentary leaf axils from which shoots will grow. There is only a short time during which they may be pruned in this way, for after the shoots begin to harden they will not develop growth buds. In nurseries it is customary to shear this Pine at the stage just described, or before growth commences. The latter method allows the uncut shoots below the sheared area to grow up beyond it, but as the older, sheared shoots do not make new growth there are often many stubs in evidence until they are hidden by the growth from below.

Common Hemlock, *Tsuga canadensis,* though a rather fast-growing tree, is quite frequently used in foundation plantings, and for this use sheared plants should be purchased, but unless the strongest shoots are pruned back every year it soon becomes too large for its position. The many kinds of Yew, *Taxus,* now used in foundation plantings usually require pruning to limit their spread. The upright Japanese Yew, *Taxus cuspidata* var. *capitata,* as received from the nursery is usually a sheared pyramid, and unless the strongest shoots which grow out over its surface are cut off each spring it soon becomes too big and looks untidy. The wide-spreading form of the same plant, known simply as *Taxus cuspidata,* grows too rapidly for foundation plantings, and the varieties *densa* and *nana,* the latter often catalogued as *brevifolia,* or some of the varieties of more recent introduction, are more suitable for foundation work, though var. *nana* needs restriction.

The numerous upright, globose, cone-shaped, or pyramidal varieties of Arborvitae, *Thuja,* and of Juniper, *Juniperus,* as a rule maintain their typical shape without great need of pruning, though the cutting back of a wayward branch is sometimes necessary, and any of them in which growth is too loose may be sheared.

Shearing is customary for any kind of coniferous hedge, and

once a year is sufficiently often unless the hedge is to be kept to a very limited size. The shearing may be done at any time from early June to August, but the earlier it is done within this period the sooner the hard, sheared outline will be covered with new growth. If a more formal appearance is preferred during the many months when there is no growth, it can be delayed to the later month.

As a rule, conifer hedges should be wider at the base than at the top, but never the reverse. The broader base allows more light to play on their sides, which aids in keeping them clothed with foliage to the ground. Yew hedges frequently, and Hemlock hedges sometimes, have vertical sides. Arborvitae is naturally rather narrow in habit and upright in growth, and when used for a hedge requires the least amount of shearing.

A narrow, cultivated strip of ground from which weeds are excluded should be maintained on each side of a hedge, for if weeds or other plants are allowed to shade the lower part of it their shade will kill the foliage of the portion in shade. Deciduous tree and shrub seedings find a suitable seedbed at the base of evergreen hedges, and must be pulled or grubbed out before they do injury.

Coniferous trees require little pruning, but occasionally, through accident or insect attack, the top of the leader, that is, the upper part of the central axis of the tree, is killed. If the injury is very near the top of the tree, one or more leaders may develop naturally, and when it can be decided which of these is the strongest the others should be cut off. If the injury is lower down and it is possible to tie one branch of the ring of branches immediately below the injury to an upright stake, it will usually become the new leader. The remaining branches of the ring must be shortened at the same time and closely watched for a year or two, and if a shoot on any one of them assumes a vertical position it also must be cut back. Unless one branch is treated in this manner, the tree may develop two or more leaders and this spoils its appearance, particularly if it is growing in a prominent position.

The branches of coniferous trees should never be heavily pruned. The most vigorous shoot and leaf growth occurs near the outer ends of the branches, the position where they receive the most light. If a branch is cut back to a point where the lateral shoots are weak through lack of sufficient light, it will be several years before new growth on these weak shoots is of near-normal proportions. And there is an equal chance that the laterals are already so weak they will die, and the whole branch with them, as conifers do not produce new shoots from dormant or adventitious buds in the manner common to deciduous trees.

Lightly pruning the branches of Pines or other coniferous trees in order to induce greater density of growth is a practice of doubtful merit. With young Pines this can be done by breaking out the central bud of the cluster of buds to be found at the end of each branch, either after the buds are fully developed in summer or before growth begins in spring. It is from this central bud that extension in the length of the branch is produced, and when it is removed the remaining buds in the cluster are forced into greater activity. Another method is to cut back to its base the one-year-old terminal shoot on each branch, that is, back to the point where the side shoots of the previous year arise. The second of these methods is useful when applied to one or more branches which may be growing too rapidly in comparison with the remainder. Sometimes young trees are pruned every year by removing the terminal bud on each branch, or at less frequent intervals by the second method, because of this desire for greater density of growth. But occasionally examples are encountered of what happens when a tree becomes too tall to be

79

readily pruned from the ground. Then the branches out of reach of the pruner are more open in growth and extend beyond those below them, which is the reverse of the natural form of these trees, with a result far from pleasing.

Sometimes the foliage of a broad-leaved evergreen or of a conifer will show brown or, as it is called, "burned" and apparently dead areas as spring advances. These vary in size from one or two shoots to the whole side of a plant. It is unwise to cut out such portions hastily or to decide a plant is completely ruined because the injury appears to be extensive. Even by cutting into some shoots for examination following recent winter injury, it is not always possible to be sure they are dead, as at this stage they may not be brown throughout and there is a reasonable chance that the injury is confined principally or entirely to the foliage. Therefore it is advisable to wait a few weeks for evidence of new growth, for if only the foliage is injured new shoots will begin to appear and no cutting will be necessary. If, on the other hand, new growth starts only on lower, older branches, it is evidence that the upper, browned parts are dead and can be cut away.

A natural phenomenon which often causes anxiety about the welfare of some conifers, particularly Arborvitaes, False-cypresses, and Junipers, is the falling in autumn of many little brown, dead twigs. This often leads to the belief that the plants are sick or dying, but it may be regarded as the equivalent of leaf fall in deciduous plants. In the examples mentioned the leaves do not drop off singly, but some of the very short, older twigs die and drop off with their small, attached dead leaves.

Evergreens, broad-leaved or conifers, are evergreen only to the extent that under suitable conditions they carry their foliage through at least one winter, but sooner or later, after one year or several, they all discard their oldest leaves.

6 The Narrow-leaved Evergreens or Conifers

Conifers are used in gardens over most of this country, though the choice is limited in regions where the annual rainfall is very low or, as in some of the plain states, where the terrain offers little natural protection from wind. Over a large part of the eastern section they have an important place in ornamental plantings, if for no other reason than that only from this group is it possible to select a variety of evergreen *trees* sufficiently hardy for the climate, and a garden of any size without some coniferous trees has a very bleak appearance in winter. With the exception of the American Holly, *Ilex opaca,* and in a more limited area one or two other tree-like Hollies, none of the broad-leaved evergreen trees can be safely grown much north of the Carolinas except in particularly favored locations, usually near the coast.

All true gardeners, however, amateur or professional, like to experiment, and no matter where they are located there will be attempts to acclimate broad-leaved and coniferous trees not considered hardy in those areas, the degree of success usually depending upon how far climatic conditions differ from those of a plant's natural environment.

As was pointed out in Chapter 1, conifers, whether trees or shrubs, lack showy flowers, but that surely is of minor importance. The Oaks, Beeches, and Elms cannot be said to be outstanding for their floral beauty, but no one would deny that these examples have other qualities which endear them to all who appreciate trees.

The attractiveness of conifers, in addition to the fact that they are evergreen and therefore ornamental the year around, is found in their varied foliage texture, differing habits of growth, and color, which may be green, blue-green, or silvery, and, though most frequently in shrub-like horticultural forms, yellow or variegated, though it is open to question whether many variegated conifers have much real merit.

Though coniferous trees are more or less pyramidal in form, they vary from the soft, loose outline of the Hemlocks, *Tsuga,* to the stiffer, sharper, almost formal shape of the Firs, *Abies.* The majority of them naturally develop an upright central trunk or axis, and deliberately shortening this axis by cutting off the upper portion ruins the tree's natural beauty, which is largely dependent upon the retention of its full height and also of the tree's lower branches so that the foliage is a flowing line from apex to ground. With increasing age it is quite normal for the lower branches to die, and their gradual removal is then necessary, but by that time a tree should have attained a height and size that make this loss seem unimportant.

Conifers are not good shade trees in the accepted meaning of that term, which implies a tree with a broad crown capable of casting a mass of shade. Whereas, being naturally broadest at the base and tapering toward the top, the amount of shade they provide in the height of summer is negligible, at least until such time as some of the lower branches must be cut away.

Evergreens, whether coniferous or broad-leaved, should not be crowded together in ornamental plantings with deciduous trees and shrubs, as close contact between the two frequently causes the shaded parts of the evergreens to die, and the dead areas become painfully obvious during the long winter months when their leafless neighbors cannot hide the injury.

A great many coniferous shrubs used in gardens are altered forms of trees. In some extreme instances these variants are completely prostrate, while others are globose, spreading, or pyramidal, and some slender and spire-like, growth patterns often far removed from that of the parent tree. These variations are usually due to seedling or bud mutations or, to use a more familiar term, they are sports.

It is a rather common assumption that all conifers are evergreen; a few, however, are deciduous. The Larches, *Larix,* are undoubtedly the most familiar examples of this small company, and the Golden Larch, *Pseudolarix amabilis,* is not uncommon. The Bald and Swamp Cypresses, *Taxodium,* of the southern United States are not so well-known in northern gardens, though they are occasionally to be found on some of the older estates. A very recent and interesting introduction from a limited area in China is Dawn Redwood, *Metasequoia glyptostroboides,* which was known only from its fossil remains until living trees were discovered a few years ago. Fortunately, importations of its seed germinated so well that it is now planted, usually in small numbers, over a wide area from southern Canada southward and westward. Another familiar tree also may be mentioned, Ginkgo or Maiden-hair Tree, *Ginkgo biloba,* a remnant of trees which, judging by the wide distribution of fossilized examples, at one period occurred widely in the northern hemisphere. Though it is not now usually included with the conifers it is closely related to them. These few, in common with other deciduous trees, lose their leaves annually in the fall of the year, therefore no further reference will be made to them.

In winter, evergreen conifers stand out in sharp contrast to their leafless deciduous neighbors, and because of this prominence they are most unsatisfactory if they are poor specimens, and have a definitely depressing effect upon the beholder. Lacking the varied and characteristic tracery of the twigs and branches of deciduous trees, ill-grown examples can offer in substitution only stunted, half-naked objects that seem to accentuate human discomfort during the bleak periods of winter. On the other hand, thrifty, well-grown conifers inspire a feeling of warmth and protection from the elements that deciduous trees cannot provide. This impression is not merely mental, as nothing will give such effective defense from searching, bitter winds as a screen of tall evergreen trees.

Sometimes the complaint is made that coniferous trees grow slowly, and while there are kinds, fortunately, of which this is true, it is not so for the majority of the commoner kinds. As a rule, they do take rather longer to become fully established after transplanting than most deciduous trees, but when this period is past, usually two or three years during which they may make only a few inches of terminal growth, given the right conditions a rate averaging a foot or more a year can be anticipated.

Because the evergreen conifers retain their leaves for several years they are not so well adapted to contend with atmospheric impurities, soot, dust, and industrial gases as deciduous trees, which, by dropping their leaves in autumn, rid themselves of much of the accumulated filth. For this reason few of the conifers are successful in or near manufacturing cities. The Yews, *Taxus,* are an exception, but they also suffer to some extent.

A word of warning may be offered to homeowners who propose to do their own foundation planting. Often knowing little of the rate of growth of trees, evergreen or deciduous, they are misled by the compactness and attractive appearance of young coniferous trees two to four feet in height and decide these are just what is required for the purpose in view. Such errors in judgment commonly include small examples of Fir, and Spruce, and sometimes of Pine. Though there are dwarf varieties of all of these trees suitable for foundation planting, they are uncommon, and when available cost many times more than the two-to-four-foot plants that to the inexperienced seem quite appropriate for their purpose. The purchasers do not realize that the rate of growth for conifers is normally quite slow during their early years, and that they have been further retarded by the necessary frequent transplanting in the nursery which is required to obtain a compact mass of roots that will make them safe to transplant without shock when they are sold.

When these young trees have been a very few years in position around the foundations of a house and are no longer subjected to periodic root disturbance, they really begin to grow, and in a surprisingly short time the lower windows of the house are hidden; and unless they are moved it does not require many more years for the upper windows also to disappear from view. In many homes some rooms are in a condition of perpetual twilight due to poor judgment in the selection of plants for foundation work. Unless these misfits are moved out to positions where they have room to develop—and this must be done before the branches on the side next to the house begin to die for lack of light—they are not worth moving, and if they are cut down the owner is faced with an expensive replacement.

PINACEAE

ABIES, "FIR." The Firs are among the most beautiful

and imposing coniferous trees but, unfortunately, they are not suitable for every location. They are very intolerant of soot and other atmospheric impurities and are, perhaps, of all conifers the least satisfactory subjects for use near towns where industrial fumes pollute the air. They are, as a rule, native to cool, moist mountain climates and are generally unsuited to low elevations, dry heat, dry soil, or exposure to high winds. For their best development they need a moist but adequately drained fertile soil, as well as clean air.

Where the environment is unsatisfactory they soon begin to show its effect by the decreased amount of annual growth, smaller leaves, and dying shoots and lower branches. Some few, however, are better adapted than others to withstand conditions not ideal to their requirements, and where Firs are to be grown purely for decorative purposes, as opposed to developing a varied collection of species, it is advisable to depend upon these tougher sorts.

The distinction between Firs and Spruces, *Picea,* causes some confusion, but the distinguishing characters of each are not hard to remember. When old Fir leaves drop off the shoots they leave circular, flat scars, and if the fingers are run along a naked shoot it feels smooth. When Spruce leaves fall they leave small, hard pegs projecting above the shoot's surface so that it is very rough to the touch. Also, cut branches of Fir hold their leaves long after the leaves are dry and brown, whereas those of Spruce fall off the cut shoot as soon as it becomes a little dry. This is one reason why Firs are preferable to Spruces as Christmas trees, but, in addition, the Firs are handsomer.

In cross section the leaves of Firs are flat, while those of Spruces are four-sided. When trees of either begin to produce cones, which requires several years, the distinction is again simple. Fir cones stand erect on the branches, and at maturity the cone scales fall away from the cone's central axis but leave the axis standing. Spruce cones hang down; the scales do not separate from the axis, but the whole cone falls.

The main branches of Firs are arranged more or less regularly in whorls or tiers around the trunk, and the distance between two definite whorls usually represents one year's extension in growth. According to kind, leaves may be green or grayish on the upper surface, and they last from eight to ten years. They arise in a spiral manner on the shoots, but in some species are so arranged that on superficial inspection they give the impression of growing out more or less horizontally from the sides and over the top of the shoot. In others they take an outward or forward and upward curve. The leaves often become gradually shorter from sides to top, and there may be a well-defined or rather indefinite V-shaped trough between the leaves of the two sides. In some species bracts project from between the cone scales and as a rule are sharply bent down over the scales. As with most of the conifers, distinguishing between one species and another is a matter of recognizing small details and requires practice.

Abies alba (*A. pectinata*), "SILVER FIR." A European tree, but not one of the best for the East, though it is frequently grown. Leaves forming a more or less distinct V depression on the upper side of the shoots, to 1 inch or a little more in length, with two white bands beneath, rounded and notched at the tip. Winter buds not resinous. Shoots gray, with scattered short hairs. Cones red-brown, to 4–5 inches long, the protruding ends of the bracts reflexed.

Abies amabilis is from northwestern North America, but not well adapted to the East. Leaves crowded, to 1¼ inches long, with two broad white bands beneath, squarish or notched at the tip. Winter buds very resinous. Shoots brownish gray, densely hairy with short, pale hairs. Cones purple, to 5 inches long.

Abies balsamea, "BALSAM FIR." Although it is native to the mountains of some eastern states and Canada, the Balsam Fir is a poor garden tree at low elevations. In its native stands, and in plantations, it is cut in great numbers for sale as Christmas trees. Leaves often forming a V depression on the upper side of the shoots, to 1 inch long, but very variable in length, with two gray bands beneath and a few lines of stomata near the tip on the upper side. Winter buds very resinous. Shoots with short, gray hairs. Cones violet-purple, to 2½ inches long, the bracts protruding or hidden.

Abies cephalonica, "GREEK FIR." The place of origin is indicated by the common name of this very ornamental Fir. Its leaves radiate around the shoots, a character it shares with *A. Pinsapo* and in which it differs from other Firs. In *A. cephalonica,* however, the leaves are rather longer and occur more thickly on the upper side of the shoots, to 1 inch long, with two white bands beneath, and occasionally with broken lines of stomata near the tip on the upper side, ending in a hard, sharp point. Winter buds resinous. Shoots shiny brown, devoid of hairs. Cones brown, to 6½ inches long, the protruding bracts reflexed.

Abies concolor, "COLORADO FIR." From the Rocky Mountains of Colorado to New Mexico. One of the best Firs for eastern gardens, and a handsome tree when soil and climate combine to suit it. Leaves to 2 inches or a little more in length, glaucous, the upper surface without a groove and with some lines of stomata, and two faint grayish bands beneath, tip rounded or with a short point. Winter buds resinous. Shoots without, or occasionally with, some very short hairs. Cones greenish or purple, to 5 inches long. The variety *violacea* has much bluer foliage.

Abies firma, "MOMI FIR." A Japanese tree with very dark green, shiny leaves, broadest near the middle, forming a V depression on the upper side of the shoots, to 1½ inches long, stiff, leathery, with two rather indefinite gray bands beneath and two sharp points at the tip. Winter buds with little resin. Shoots slightly grooved, and short-hairy in the grooves. Cones light green, to 4½ inches long, the projecting bracts reflexed. Young trees of this Fir were considerably injured in the exceptionally severe winter of 1933–34 in Yonkers, New York.

Abies Fraseri, "FRASER FIR." This Fir has a rather limited distribution in the Allegheny Mountains and nearby areas, and considerable similarity to *A. balsamea,* and some to *A. Veitchii,* and though it is a better garden tree in the East than the former, it is not so satisfactory as *A. Veitchii.* Leaves often forming a V depression on the upper side of the shoots, to 1 inch long, with two broad white bands beneath and with more stomatic lines on the upper surface near the tip than in *A. balsamea,* tip notched. Winter buds very resinous. Shoots thickly covered with short reddish hairs. Cones purple, to 2½ inches long, the projecting scales reflexed.

Abies grandis, "GIANT FIR," is from western North America, and as it is not quite sufficiently hardy and prefers a cooler, moister summer climate, it is not one of the best for the East. Leaves shiny, to 2 inches or a little more in length, with two white bands beneath, notched at the tip. Winter buds resinous. Shoots green, the short hairs falling away early. Cones green, to 4 inches long.

Abies homolepis (*A. brachyphylla*), "NIKKO FIR." From Japan, this one grows well in eastern gardens. Leaves forming a V depression on the upper side of the shoots, to 1 inch long, with two broad white bands beneath, and notched at the tip. Winter buds resinous. Shoots markedly grooved, but without hairs. Cones purple, to 4 inches long.

Abies koreana, "KOREAN FIR." Though not yet common, this handsome Fir is doing well in the East. Leaves crowded to ¾ inch long, shiny, broadest toward the apex, with two broad, very white bands beneath, and notched or sometimes pointed at the tip. Winter buds slightly resinous. Shoots at first sparingly hairy, becoming naked. Cones bluish purple, to 2½ inches long, the projecting bracts reflexed. Korea.

Abies lasiocarpa, "ROCKY MOUNTAIN FIR." Plants of this western Fir are variable in behavior, but it is not generally one of the best for the East. Leaves bluish green, to 1½ inches long, with two broad grayish bands beneath, and lines of stomata on the upper surface, tip rounded or short-pointed. Winter buds resinous. Shoots gray, covered with short reddish hairs. Cones purple, to 4 inches long.

Abies magnifica, "RED FIR." From Oregon and California, this one forms a narrow, handsome pyramid which grows quite well in the East. Leaves to 1¾ inches long, glaucous, with two grayish bands beneath and lines of stomata on the upper side but, contrary to the general rule among Firs, somewhat four-sided rather than flat, so the upper surface appears to bear a longitudinal ridge in place of the groove common to many of them. Winter buds resinous. Shoots covered with short, reddish hairs. Cones violet-purple, to 9 inches long.

Abies Nordmanniana, "NORDMANN FIR." From the shores of the Black Sea and the Caucasus, it is among the best for eastern gardens. Leaves thickly set, to 1¼ inches long, upper surface shiny, with two white bands beneath, and notched at the tip. Winter buds not resinous. Shoots with short scattered hairs. Cones dark brown, to 6 inches long, the bracts projecting a little beyond the scales, and reflexed.

Abies numidica "ALGERIAN FIR," is not one of the har-

Abies Veitchii, ''VEITCH FIR''

diest and should be provided with protection from cold winds. Leaves to ¾ inch long, with two white bands beneath and some lines of stomata on the upper surface near the tip, tip rounded or notched. Winter buds usually without or with a small amount of resin. Shoots brown, without hairs. Cones reddish, to 7 inches long. Algeria.

Abies Pinsapo, "SPANISH FIR." Very distinct, and peculiar for the manner in which the short leaves radiate around the shoots. Leaves stiff, to ¾ inch long, grayish, with stomatic lines on the upper surface and two pale gray bands beneath, short-pointed or blunt at the tip. Winter buds resinous. Shoots smooth or shallowly grooved, without hairs. Cones purplish, to 4½ inches long. Spain.

Abies procera (*A. nobilis*), "NOBLE FIR." Another tree usually satisfactory in eastern conditions, and generally similar to and sometimes confused with *A. magnifica.* The leaves of *A. procera,* however, have a groove on the upper surface in place of the ridge in *A. magnifica,* and they average a little shorter, to 1¼ inches, and are set more thickly on the shoots. They have two grayish bands on the lower surface and some lines of stomata on the upper, and are rounded or occasionally notched at the tip. Winter buds resinous. Shoots covered with rusty-brown hairs. Cones purplish, to 10 inches long, the reflexed bracts covering the greater part of the scales. Pacific Northwest.

Abies Veitchii, "VEITCH FIR." This very ornamental Japanese tree grows well in the East and is one of the most pleasing. Leaves closely set on the shoots, to 1 inch long, very shiny above and with two very white bands beneath, and blunt-pleasing. Leaves closely set on the shoots, to 1 inch long, very resinous. Shoots more or less short-hairy. Cones bluish purple, to 2½ inches long, the bracts slightly extended and reflexed.

There are a number of other Firs, some of more recent introduction and neither widely tested nor distributed, and other older ones poorly adapted to the East.

PINACEAE

Biota orientalis. A synonym of *Thuja orientalis,* Oriental Arborvitae, but the name still rather frequently used in nursery catalogues for that plant and varieties of it.

PINACEAE

CEDRUS, ''CEDAR.'' The trees in this genus are the true Cedars, of which the best known by name is the biblical Cedar of Lebanon, but as occurs with some other common names Cedar is used for plants in other genera. Notable among these are: Red Cedar, *Juniperus virginiana;* White Cedar, *Chamaecyparis thyoides;* Incense Cedar, *Libocedrus decurrens,* and several others.

Cedars produce two kinds of shoot—one is very short and spur-like with a negligible growth in length each year on which the leaves are very closely spaced. The other kind is a normal shoot in the common meaning of the word, which serves to increase the size and density of the tree by extending the length of the branches and of some of their side shoots. On the latter kind of shoot the leaves arise spirally and with a well-marked interval between them. The same kinds of shoot growth occur in the Larches, *Larix,* but their leaves are deciduous.

Cedars are not readily transplanted unless they have been frequently moved or root-pruned in the nursery. They require a well-drained soil on the sandy side, and no attempt should be made to force growth in any way or the plant may become too soft and, consequently, more liable to winter injury. Cedar trees are broadly pyramidal in outline for many years, but may eventually develop massive, wide-spreading branches, though this is hardly likely to occur in one lifetime.

Cedrus atlantica, "ATLAS CEDAR." This species and *C. libani* differ so little from one another that it is difficult to separate them. Indeed, by some botanists all the Cedars are considered to be different forms of one species, but principally because of their geographical distribution it is usually regarded as desirable to recognize them as distinct species. *C. atlantica* has leaves 1 inch or less in length, and quite frequently they are glaucous-green. The shoots are covered with short, soft hairs, usually more densely than in *C. libani*, which may be without hairs. Cones to 3 inches high and 2 inches broad. This Cedar originates in Algeria and Morocco, and is doubtfully hardy north of New York City. But there is a variety of it, *glauca*, which is hardier and quite extensively grown in that area. This is a striking plant, readily distinguishable by its blue-gray leaves.

Cedrus Deodara, "DEODAR." This Himalayan species is much more tender than either of the others, but a very beautiful subject. As a young tree it is without their stiffness, as the leading shoot and branches droop gracefully. It has longer, grayer leaves, to 1½ inches or rather more, and soft-hairy shoots. Cones 3–4 inches long and 2½ inches broad. Here again its var. *glauca* seems to be somewhat hardier than the parent.

Cedrus libani, "CEDAR OF LEBANON." The hardiest, and for its scriptural associations the most famous, Cedar, but as already explained differing little from *C. atlantica* except in its slightly longer, to 1¼ inches, green leaves and usually naked, but sometimes sparingly hairy, shoots, and larger cones, to 4½ inches long by 2½ inches broad. Asia Minor and Syria.

TAXACEAE

CEPHALOTAXUS, "PLUM-YEW." Large shrubs in cultivation, though said to be trees in their native lands. In general appearance they suggest long-leaved Yews and like them are tolerant of shade, but they have a more open habit of growth and two longitudinal white bands on the underside of the leaves in place of the pale green ones of Yew. The Plum-like fruits require two years to develop.

Cephalotaxus drupacea is from Japan, and a large shrub widely but openly branched. Leaves to about 1½ inches long, with two broad whitish bands beneath, ending in a short but not hard point, and, though originating spirally, arranged in two ranks often forming a narrow V-shaped channel on the upper side of the shoots. The egg-shaped "plums" are green, about 1 inch long. A variety, *fastigiata,* has the branches upright in growth and, consequently, is a much narrower plant, and its leaves radiate around the shoots; they are not in two ranks. However, it is not so hardy as the species. Another variety, *pedunculata,* Harrington Plum-Yew, has leaves intermediate in length, to 2 inches, between *C. drupacea* and *C. Fortunii,* but it has the greater hardiness of the former. It has been suggested that this variety is a hybrid of the two, as wild plants are not known, though it is said to be much cultivated in Japan.

Cephalotaxus Fortunii is a Chinese plant, more compact and shrub-like in growth than *C. drupacea,* but also irregularly branched. Leaves 2–3 inches long, tapering to a point, arranged in two almost horizontal ranks and frequently curved. Not so hardy as *C. drupacea,* and with purple fruits.

95

CHAMAECYPARIS, "FALSE-CYPRESS." It is now fairly well-accepted practice to use the name "False-cypress" for this group of plants which was formerly included with Cypress, *Cupressus,* though the older common name is still frequently used. For example: Lawson Cypress, *Chamaecyparis Lawsoniana;* Hinoki Cypress, *Chamaecyparis obtusa;* Sawara Cypress, *Chamaecyparis pisifera,* and others. A further cause of confusion is the name *Retinispora* or *Retinospora,* which is also sometimes used for some of the *Chamaecyparis,* but more particularly for the juvenile forms of *C. obtusa* and *C. pisifera.*

The False-cypresses are among those conifers with very small, scale-like leaves closely pressed to the shoots, except in those varieties with juvenile foliage, in which case their longer leaves project away from the shoots, a feature which gives distinction to a number of them. Some very ornamental and popular shrubs are included among the False-cypresses, and in one quality at least they are superior to most varieties of the American Arbor-vitae, *Thuja occidentalis,* as they do not assume the often rather dingy brownish green shades common to the latter in winter. They require a slightly acid, moist soil, and should not be placed in positions exposed to strong winds. Their small cones are of questionable ornamental value.

Chamaecyparis Lawsoniana, "LAWSON FALSE-CYPRESS." A native of Oregon and northern California and of doubtful hardiness much north of New York City, except near the coast. Pyramidal in outline, with bright green foliage arranged in somewhat horizontal, drooping sprays, it is the handsomest of the False-cypresses. In Great Britain and the milder parts of Europe, with its numerous varieties it outranks in popularity all other False-cypresses. Unfortunately, many of its very

Abies pinsapo, "SPANISH FIR"

Daphne cneorum, "ROSE DAPHNE"

Nandina domestica, "CHINESE SACRED BAMBOO"

Chamaecyparis Lawsoniana Allumii, ''SCARAB FALSE-CYPRESS''

attractive varieties are not sufficiently hardy for the Northeast, but those which follow seem to be among the most reliable. Var. *Allumii* is a columnar plant with bluish foliage; var. *argentea* has much more silvery foliage; var. *Stewartii* is a very striking yellow-foliaged plant, particularly the new growth, but the color becomes somewhat less pronounced as the season advances; var. Triomphe de Boskoop is one of the hardiest and best for steel-blue foliage color.

Chamaecyparis nootkatensis, "NOOTKA FALSE-CYPRESS." This is another species from northwestern America, but it has never acquired great popularity. Its foliage lacks the brightness of *C. Lawsoniana,* though the plant is much hardier. Of a limited number of varieties, two are worth noting. Var. *glauca* has grayish glaucous foliage and is a dense and rather slow-growing shrub. Var. *pendula* has horizontal branches, and the branchlets hang vertically. It is of a medium rate of growth and is one of the most outstanding weeping conifers, though its extreme weeping habit may appear rather too mournful to suit some tastes.

Chamaecyparis obtusa, "HINOKI FALSE-CYPRESS." A Japanese species, some of the varieties of which are very popular in eastern gardens, much more so than the species itself, though the latter makes a horizontally branched tree of quite attractive appearance. Of its varieties, *compacta* is a slow-growing, dense form; var. *Crippsii* is a handsome golden-foliaged plant, narrowly pyramidal in shape; var. *ericoides*, a rounded, dense bush with juvenile foliage, that is, the short, pointed leaves project from the shoots, and the foliage turns purple in fall but becomes green again with the increasing warmth of the following spring; of very slow growth and requiring protection from cold winds; var. *filicoides* has an irregular outline, but short, attractive, fern-like shoots; var. *gracilis* is among the best and is widely grown. Though it grows into a large shrub it does so relatively slowly. It is pyramidal, with the shoots appearing cupped at the outer ends. There is also a golden-foliaged form of it, *gracilis aurea*. Var. *lycopodioides* is, perhaps, more of an oddity than a thing of beauty, as it is not very regular in habit and has thickened, often pendulous shoots, clubbed or fasciated at the ends. Again there is a rarer golden-foliaged form, *lycopodioides aurea*. A very slow-growing variety is *nana* (*nana gracilis*) which, though not unlike *gracilis*, has a very much slower rate of increase in size. This one and the golden form, *nana aurea*, are well adapted to use in the rock garden.

Chamaecyparis pisifera, "SAWARA FALSE-CYPRESS." This is also from Japan, but does not grow into such an ornamental tree as *C. obtusa*, as it is too prone to become thinly furnished with foliage in spite of its abundant branches. Like *C. obtusa* it has provided a multitude of garden varieties, but, broadly speaking, they are of more rapid growth and generally coarser than the varieties of *C. obtusa*. Too many foundation plantings have been overgrown with them which would have been satisfactory for many more years had some of the more suitable varieties of *C. obtusa* been chosen. There is a yellow- or golden-foliaged form of it, *C. pisifera aurea*, but it does not hold its color well. Var. *filifera* is a broad-based, pyramidal shrub with long, thin, cord-like, pendulous shoots, and is among the best of the *C. pisifera* varieties, though in sharp contrast to plants more normally upright or spreading in habit. It is usually listed under the imposing common name of Thread Sawara False-cypress. It has a golden-foliaged form, *filifera aurea*. Var. *plumosa* is usually conical in outline, with pretty, fern-like, juvenile foliage, but, like the parent species, is apt to become thin in appearance unless pruned or sheared; *plumosa aurea* is its golden-foliaged form. Var. *plumosa flavescens* is much paler in color than the last, the young growth often a whitish yellow, denser, and of slower growth. Var. *squarrosa* will grow into a very attractive small tree, but is more often seen as a shrub of varying size. However, it is very apt to become unshapely unless some corrective pruning is done for a number of years. It is very tolerant of shearing, and too often is "barbered" into a misshapen monstrosity because it was chosen for a foundation planting or other restricted position without realization of its rapid rate of growth. It has bluish, soft, feathery, juvenile foliage, the leaves projecting about ¼ inch.

Chamaecyparis thyoides, "WHITE FALSE-CYPRESS." This is the hardiest of the False-cypresses and an eastern American native of swampy ground, but not considered sufficiently ornamental for garden use where the better kinds may be grown. Of a few varieties, *andelyensis* is probably the most interesting. This is a slow-growing, upright shrub of pyramidal outline, with short secondary shoots, and usually bearing both adult and juvenile foliage, but it is not quite so hardy as the parent species.

PINACEAE

CRYPTOMERIA. The genus is represented by the one species given here.

Cryptomeria japonica, "CRYPTOMERIA." A handsome Japanese tree with noticeably red-brown bark and spreading or drooping branches, the small leaves somewhat vertically flattened so that the edges are on the upper and lower sides, curved, pointing forward, and radiating around the shoots, the earliest spring leaves shorter than those coming later, which are about ½ inch long. Cones round, about ¾ inch in diameter. The variety *Lobbii* is hardier than the type, and a more compact, denser tree, and is the form which seems to be most frequently grown.

Cryptomeria japonica, "CRYPTOMERIA"

C. japonica has produced a number of shrubby varieties which find a limited use in gardens, but all of them probably more tender than var. *Lobbii.* Var. *dacrydioides* is usually a compact shrub with thin, rather short branchlets and short leaves. Var. *elegans* is quite striking, as it is densely branched, has longer, slimmer, light green leaves, to 1 inch long, which turn bronzy in winter. Var. *nana* is a low, compact, slow-growing plant. Var. *Vilmoriniana* is a very small, mound-like, dense plant with many little branches and very small leaves, and best adapted to the rock garden. Var. *sinensis* is from China, and much more tender than *C. japonica.* There are other varieties.

PINACEAE

CUNNINGHAMIA. A genus of two species, the second one, *C. Konishii,* very rare and still more tender.

Cunninghamia lanceolata. This Chinese tree is not rare in the Northeast, though it is not quite sufficiently hardy much north of Virginia except in very favored positions. The examples encountered frequently have two or more stems in place of the normal single one. Closer inspection usually shows a stump, indicating that these plants have been killed to the ground at some time, perhaps more than once, which accounts for the multiple stems. Because of this ability, rare in conifers, to sprout from the stump, it is worth giving a trial in a sheltered position, as it is a very distinct and pleasing tree if it reaches a height of 20 feet or more. The leaves are very closely spaced in two more or less horizontal ranks, but the upper sides of the shoots are generally hidden by them, and actually they originate in a spiral manner. They are variable in size to about 2¼ inches long, shiny, bluish green above, with two broad white bands beneath, and with fine teeth on their margins, and gradually tapering to a needle-like point. Cones nearly round, to about 1½ inches long.

PINACEAE

CUPRESSUS, "CYPRESS." The true Cypresses are not sufficiently hardy for the Northeast, the majority of them being better adapted to areas south of Virginia or to California. One of them, however, the Californian *C. Macnabiana,* may grow precariously further north if it is given a sheltered position. It is then little more than a shrub and has very small scale-like leaves.

Visitors to the Mediterranean coast of Italy and France are usually impressed by the upright, very narrow Cypress grown in great numbers in that region, and enquire whether it could be grown in northeastern America. The plant in question is the variety *stricta* of *C. sempervirens,* which forms a tall, very narrow column; it is not sufficiently hardy north of the Carolinas, but is common in California.

PINACEAE

JUNIPERUS, "JUNIPER." A genus of evergreen trees and shrubs of the northern hemisphere. Not all of them, however, are hardy in the Northeast, but from among those which are hardy and their varieties—and some of the more important of these follow—trees, shrubs of various sizes and growth habits, and ground covers may be selected.

As a rule the hardy Junipers will succeed in a drier, poorer soil than is required by most other conifers, but nevertheless a better response is to be expected from more generous treatment, and while the majority of them seem to prefer soils containing lime, the latter condition is not essential. Of various insect pests likely to attack them, there are two which are not readily detected that will cause disfigurement and great injury if they are not rigidly controlled. These are scale insects and red spider mites, but the use of a miticide or a dormant season oil or lime-sulfur spray will control them, though oils must not be used on Junipers having principally awl-like leaves, or lime-sulfur near painted structures.

Junipers have two kinds of leaves, either small and scale-like and generally closely pressed to the shoots, or larger and awl- or needle-like and standing out from the shoots. Some Junipers have awl-like leaves in rings of three on all shoots, while in others they are in threes only on the leading shoots, but in opposite pairs elsewhere. Or the leaves may be almost entirely scale-like, but with some little shoots bearing awl-like leaves in pairs or threes. Leaves may also be jointed at the point of union with the shoot, or they may be decurrent, that is, the leaf bases are prolonged down the shoot.

Juniperus chinensis, "CHINESE JUNIPER." This plant from China, Japan, and Mongolia has provided gardens with a number of shrubby forms in addition to being ornamental as a small tree. When plants are raised from imported seed they vary in outline from rather narrow pyramidal to columnar, and some of the latter have a very narrow form. The foliage is glaucous-green, and both scale-like and awl-like leaves usually are present, with the latter in threes or opposite, their bases extending down the shoot, and the upper sides of the leaves with two grayish bands. The berries are covered with a heavy white bloom.

The following are some of its varieties: *aurea,* an erect plant with the young growth golden; *foemina* (*Reevesii*), an upright female form of light green color, with scale-like leaves. Var. *globosa* is a low shrub roughly circular in outline when viewed from above, but hardy globose. It grows rather slowly, has principally scale-like leaves, and is suitable for a restricted position. Var. *japonica* is a low, spreading, ground-cover plant with short upright shoots from its prostrate stems, with awl-like leaves predominating. A colored form of it, *japonica aureo-*

Juniperus chinensis Pfitzeriana, "PFITZER JUNIPER"

Juniperus chinensis Sargentii.

variegata, has principally golden foliage. Var. *mas* is a dense, upright, pyramidal male form which bears quantities of tiny flower masses in spring. Var. *Pfitzeriana* probably is the commonest of the varieties of *J. chinensis* and a most attractive plant. The branches spread outward and upward, and the branchlets droop. Eventually it becomes a very large shrub, but if kept free of insects remains handsome. A much lower and rather smaller form of it, *Pfitzeriana compacta,* grows more slowly, and with the branches more nearly horizontal at a foot or two above the ground. In contrast to *Pfitzeriana,* which retains a good green color through the winter, this smaller form assumes a purplish tinge. Var. *plumosa* is another low, spreading shrub, with drooping tips to its short, upright branchlets, and there is a golden-foliaged form of it, *plumosa aurea*. Var. *pyramidalis* is composed of almost upright branches, and has a rather formal, narrowly pyramidal shape. Var. *Sargentii* has become quite popular as one of the taller ground covers. Its stems are prostrate with upright branches to about 1½ feet which eventually form a dense, broad mass of growth. Var. *variegata* is an oval, upright shrub on which many of the shoot tips are white.

Juniperus communis, "COMMON JUNIPER." In its wild state this Juniper has a wide distribution in Europe and northern Asia, and some in North America. It is variable in habit depending upon its place of origin, but is more often shrubby than tree-like, and attains the latter size very slowly. Young shoots triangular, leaves awl-shaped, their bases jointed, three at a joint, sharp-pointed, with a broad white band along the upper surface. Some of its varieties are: *aurea,* the young leaves and shoots golden, later turning green; var. *aureo-spica* is a popular garden plant because of its golden foliage and rather low stature. The shoots rise to about 2 feet from trailing branches, but it remains dense. Var. *depressa* (*canadensis*) reaches a height of 3–4 feet from trailing branches and will eventually cover a large area. It is a useful plant as a tall ground cover for rough places, but a little too coarse for the average garden. Var. *hibernica,* Irish Juniper, is a densely branched, fastigiate shrub useful for a formal position, but it is a little more prone to winter injury than the very similar Swedish Juniper, var. *suecica*. Var. *oblongo-pendula* is a much broader shrub with upright stems and pendulous branchlets which give the plant a very graceful appearance. Var. *saxatilis* (*montana*), Mountain Juniper, is another low, mat-like shrub with trailing branches and upright shoots of 1 foot or a little more in height. As one plant may eventually cover an area 10–12 feet in diameter, it makes an excellent ground cover for banks. Var. *suecica*, Swedish Juniper, is, as already mentioned, very similar to the Irish Juniper, but grows a little more slowly, is rather narrower in outline, and the extreme ends of its shoots droop, whereas they are upright in the Irish Juniper. A form of it, *suecica nana*, is smaller in its parts and grows still more slowly.

Juniperus conferta (*J. litoralis*), "SHORE JUNIPER." Japan. Another low, wide-spreading shrub, with branchlets rising about 1 foot above the ground. It has almost ½-inch, awl-like leaves in threes, their bases jointed, and with a narrow white band and a groove along the upper side, usually a lighter green than varieties of *J. communis*, but otherwise very similar in appearance. An excellent ground-cover plant for large areas.

Juniperus horizontalis, "CREEPING JUNIPER." A northern North American species which, along with some of its varieties, is a very useful low ground cover. *J. horizontalis* is completely prostrate, though the younger branches spread over the older ones. The young foliage is light green, and the mature foliage blue-green. Both scale- and awl-like leaves are usually present, the latter in opposite pairs, their bases extending down the shoot. A popular steel-blue form of it is called Bar Harbor Juniper. Its var. *alpina* is totally different in habit, as the branches rise to 2–3 feet from stems which gradually bend toward the ground. It is a rather loose but distinctive plant with small, ⅕-inch, awl-like leaves, blue-gray in color. Var. *Douglasii*, Waukegan Juniper, is another trailing plant notable for its blue summer color which turns purplish in winter. Var. *glauca* differs from *J. horizontalis* only in its whiter, glaucous foliage. Var. *plumosa*, Andorra Juniper, is a spreading shrub with crested, flattened ends to its 1½-foot upright shoots arising from horizontal stems.

Juniperus procumbens. Another spreading plant from Japan which makes an excellent ground cover 12–18 inches high, with upright shoots from trailing stems. Its awl-shaped leaves are about ⅓ inch long, in threes, their bases prolonged down the shoot, with the white band on the upper surface divided for only part of its length by the green midrib, and on the under side two white spots at the base of each leaf. The young shoots glaucous.

Juniperus rigida. A small Asiatic tree, but in cultivation more frequently a large shrub broadly pyramidal when young, with drooping, ridged, and glaucous branchlets. Leaves awl-shaped, to ¾ inch long, in threes, jointed at the base, and a deep groove and narrow white band along the center. An interesting Juniper of quite dense growth, the leaves remarkably long though very similar in general appearance to the shorter ones of *J. communis.*

Juniperus Sabina, "SAVIN." A pretty, slow-growing, spreading rather than upright, shrub, the leaves principally scale-like, and when awl-shaped leaves are present they are opposite and extending down the shoot, the upper surface glaucous and with a pronounced midrib, and the under surface green. In the wild state it is said to occur in limestone regions, which may account for its sometimes unsatisfactory behavior in acid soils. If the foliage is crushed it has an unpleasant odor. Its var. *fastigiata* is an upright plant of dark green color and principally scale-like leaves. The best-known variety is *tamariscifolia,* which is a favorite garden plant with almost horizontally spreading branches and preponderantly awl-shaped leaves.

Juniperus scopulorum, "WESTERN RED CEDAR." This tree is very similar to the Eastern Red Cedar, *J. virginiana,* but is a western native which may eventually become a small, round-topped tree; in the young state it has a columnar habit similar to that of its eastern counterpart. In very young plants acicular

Juniperus Sabina tamariscifolia.

leaves predominate and the foliage is usually of a brighter bluish green than that of *J. virginiana*. The berries require two years to ripen, while those of the eastern plant ripen in one. Its var. *argentea* has much more silvery foliage than the type. Var. *horizontalis* is a rather narrow, upright form with short horizontal branches and silvery foliage; and var. *viridifolia* is a rather broader, green-foliaged, pyramidal plant.

Juniperus squamata. An Asiatic plant with prostrate stems and short ascending shoots which are green and grooved. The small, bluish green leaves are awl-shaped and in threes, and usually more or less pressed against the shoot with their bases prolonged down the shoot. The upper surface is divided by a narrow, green midrib, and the green underside has a groove along its center.

Juniperus virginiana, "EASTERN RED CEDAR." This is the Juniper common to a large part of the eastern United States, often seen in great numbers on poor fields and hillsides in all sizes from small seedlings to rather narrowly pyramidal or columnar trees, but in the South with a much wider head and more horizontally spreading branches. On young plants the leaves are awl-shaped, in threes, their bases prolonged down the shoot, with a broad gray band along the upper surface; when present on older plants these leaves are more often opposite, but scale-like leaves appear in increasing numbers until they soon predominate. Another common name for this plant is Pencil Cedar, as its straight-grained wood is favored for pencil manufacture. In addition, it is highly valued for fence posts and similar purposes, as it is straight, and long-lasting in the ground.

Red Cedar is an ornamental garden plant when it is well branched to the base, but usually some of its varieties, of which there are many good ones, are used in preference. Var. *Canaertii* forms a closely branched pyramid, with bright green, mostly scale-like leaves and glaucous berries generously produced. Var. *elegantissima* has the shoot tips golden yellow, is also pyramidal in habit, but is more loosely branched. Var. *glauca* makes a tall column attractively gray-glaucous in color, the leaves scale-like. Var. *globosa* grows rather slowly, and is a dense, rounded shrub with scale-like, dark green leaves. Var. *Keteleeri* is a handsome, broadly pyramidal plant which eventually will become very tall. Var. *Kosteri* is low in stature, but the branches spread widely, and the foliage is glaucous and principally scale-like. Var. *pendula* is rather thinly branched, with horizontal branches and drooping branchlets and scale-like leaves. Ornamentally it is a rather pleasing contrast to the many varieties of denser, upright habit. Var. *pyramidalis* is more nearly columnar in shape. Var. *Schottii* is light green in color, and of columnar form, with scale-like leaves. Var. *tripartita* becomes a very large shrub with a broad top from a narrow base, and has awl-like leaves of good green color.

LIBOCEDRUS. There are several known species of this plant, but few of them in cultivation, and of these the one given below is the hardiest.

Libocedrus decurrens, "INCENSE CEDAR." This tree from the western United States is not often seen in eastern gardens. In New Jersey there is a magnificent specimen approximately 80–90 feet tall, which, about a hundred years ago, may have been the first of its kind brought to the East. Incense Cedar has a somewhat stiffly formal outline, and quite small trees show this character. This is due to the great number of consistently short branches which grow from the trunk and terminate in many vertical, flattened branchlets, so that the tree is densely columnar in shape. Leaves small and scale-like, dark green. The tree is of doubtful hardiness, however, much north of New York City, except near the coast, and should be planted in a protected position.

PICEA, "SPRUCE." The most readily noted distinctions between Spruce and Fir were pointed out under the latter. The Spruces are shallow-rooted trees and are generally more tolerant of wet soils than either Firs or Pines, so they should not be planted in ground that is very sandy or naturally dry. The hardier kinds are much more tolerant of exposure to wind than the Firs.

The Spruces, along with the Firs, Hemlocks, and Pines, are decorative garden trees, and where atmospheric conditions are suitable to all of them, the final choice in some instances may well depend upon the type of soil. The commoner Spruces may be used for hedges and, if the base of the hedge is kept free of weed growth and it is always sheared to maintain a greater width at the base than at the top, will form a very close living fence, pleasing in appearance.

Like the Firs and Pines, the Spruces produce their branches in whorls or rings around the trunk, each complete whorl representing one year's growth. The leaves arise spirally on the shoots, and in most species are quadrangular in cross section, with lines of stomata on all four surfaces. In a few, however, the leaves are more flattened, with stomatic lines on only the two sides which form the lower surface.

Two kinds of Spruce gall aphid are disfiguring and injurious to these trees. The injury appears as woody, cone-like growths, often in great numbers, either at the base of new shoots for one kind of gall aphid, or toward the end of the shoots for the other. Where the trees are small and the galls few in number, they should be cut off and burned as soon as detected, but for larger trees where hand picking is not practicable, they should be sprayed just before growth commences in spring, the spraying to be repeated in fall if there is a heavy aphid infestation. Information giving the proper times for these spray applications can be obtained from the state experiment station. Malathion, or a nicotine and soap solution applied with force, or a miscible oil spray at the correct dilution for conifers are all effective, but oils will destroy for a time the bloomy coating on the foliage of Blue Spruce. Spruce mite, one of the "red spiders," is another common and very injurious pest for which a miticide should be used.

Picea Abies (*P. excelsa*), "NORWAY SPRUCE." This Spruce has been more extensively planted in eastern gardens than any other. Its greatest fault is that with age it does not often make a good-looking tree, but young trees are very pleasing. Its leaves are quadrangular, dark green, to about ¾ inch long. Shoots brown, without or rarely with some downy hairs. Cones purple or green, to 6 inches long.

The Norway Spruce has given rise to a great many varieties; some of these are trees, of which a few have peculiar habits of growth, while others are mere shrubs, usually very dense in habit, with differences in rate of growth and size of leaf. It is not unusual for one or more shoots in these dwarf forms to revert to the tree-like habit of Norway Spruce if they are not cut out as soon as detected.

Of the tree forms of *P. Abies,* two are quite interesting but uncommon, and in no sense offensive, as are some colored conifers. Var. *argenteo-spica* has white tips to the young spring growth, and seen at a little distance gives the impression that the tree is covered with small white blossoms, but these white tips soon begin to turn green. The other is var. *finedonensis,* in which the young shoots are yellow, later turning green. Other tree-forming varieties of interest are: *columnaris,* which is well described by its name, as it forms a densely branched, narrow, columnar tree with short horizontal branches. Var. *cupressina* is a rather narrow pyramid, but in this instance the short branches are more nearly upright.

There are also some pendulous forms, and of these var. *inversa* has weeping branches which produce an abundance of long, thin, pendulous branchlets. Var. *pendula* also has pendulous branches, but not quite to the extreme degree of those of *inversa,* as they stand out a little further from the trunk and they are not so generously provided with branchlets. In vigorous plants of either of the above the lower branches may spread over the ground. A curiosity rather than a thing of beauty is var. *virgata,* as it has many fewer than the normal complement of branches, which usually take a downward curve but are by no means consistent in that respect, and these may be nearly completely, or sometimes completely, destitute of side shoots. There are a number of other tree-like forms.

Many dwarf varieties of *P. Abies* are recognized, but as the distinctions between one variety and another are often small, there has been a considerable amount of confusion of names. Comparatively few of these dwarf forms are carried by American nurserymen, which is to be accounted for by their slow rate of growth. Some may reach a height of 3 feet and a diameter half again as great in from fifteen to twenty years, while other still lower-growing kinds may be no more than a foot or so high and 2–3 feet in width in the same period of time, a size so small that few are willing to pay what the nurseryman must charge to cover the cost of the years of care. The following are some of those most frequently grown:

Clanbrasiliana	*nana*
Ellwangeriana	*Parsonsii*
Gregoryana	*procumbens*
Maxwellii	*pygmaea*
mucronata	*Remontii*

Picea bicolor (*P. Alcockiana*), "ALCOCK SPRUCE." A pleasing, rather slow-growing Japanese tree. Leaves to ¾ inch long, dark green, with five or six stomatic lines on the two upper surfaces, and usually two on each lower one. Shoots whitish the first year, later turning pale brown, usually somewhat short-hairy. Cones purple, to 4 inches long.

Picea Engelmannii, "ENGELMANN SPRUCE." A splendid Spruce from western North America that grows well in the

Northeast. Leaves glaucous-green, to 1 inch long, rather thin and flexible, and of unpleasant odor when bruised. Shoots grayish yellow, with minute scattered hairs. Cones tinged red, to 2½ inches long.

Picea glauca (*P. alba, P. canadensis*), "WHITE SPRUCE." A native of northern North America and distributed across the continent. A good garden tree as well as being immensely important for its timber. Leaves grayish or bluish green, to ¾ inch long, with an unpleasant odor when bruised, which has given rise to another common name, Skunk Spruce. Shoots drooping, pale brown, without down. Cones green, to 2 inches long. Its var. *conica* is a slow-growing, exceedingly dense shrub with crowded, thin shoots, and thin, light green leaves about ½ inch long. This variety is quite popular in gardens but is very subject to attack by spider mites, and unless these are rigidly kept in check the plant is soon discolored and much of the foliage killed.

Picea Glehnii, "SAGHALIN SPRUCE." From Saghalin Island and Japan. A rather slow-growing and narrowly pyramidal Spruce of pleasing appearance. Shoots reddish brown, densely short-hairy, but sometimes only in the grooves. Winter buds resinous. Cones violet, to 3 inches long.

Picea mariana (*P. nigra*), "BLACK SPRUCE." A northern North American species, but at low elevations not satisfactory as a garden plant. It grows rather slowly and has a narrow outline. Leaves bluish or glaucous green, to ¾ inch long. Shoots brownish, densely covered with short glandular hairs. Cones purple, to 1¼ inches long, not falling for some years after they mature. The smaller var. *Doumetii* is a much better garden plant but of slower growth and much denser habit.

Picea Omorika, "SERVIAN SPRUCE." One of the best and handsomest Spruces for the East, from a limited area in Yugoslavia. A very beautiful plant as it increases in size, the branches drooping, then curving outward, and the foliage of a

Picea Omorika, "SERVIAN SPRUCE"

very attractive grayish shade. Leaves flattened, ½–¾ inch long, shiny green on the upper surface, silvery gray on the lower, due to two broad stomatic bands. Shoots light brown, and short-hairy. Cones bluish purple, to 2 inches long. Var. *pendula* has a very much more pronounced drooping habit.

Picea orientalis, "ORIENTAL SPRUCE." One of the prettiest and best; its very shiny, short, closely set leaves immediately call attention to it, but it grows rather slowly. Leaves dark green, about ½ inch long, blunt-ended. Shoots pale brown, densely short-hairy. Cones purple, to 3½ inches long. From Asia Minor and the Caucasus.

Picea polita, "TIGERTAIL SPRUCE." Japan. Another ornamental species which grows well in the East. Peculiar for its shiny, dark green, hard, spine-tipped leaves, about ¾ inch long. Shoots rather thick, pale yellow, without down. Cones yellow-green, to 4 inches long.

Picea pungens (*P. Parryana*), "COLORADO SPRUCE," "BLUE SPRUCE." From Colorado, Utah, and other Mountain States. This Spruce and some of its varieties are very popular in the East, and are among the most suitable for the region. Collectively, they are much more commonly referred to as Blue Spruce than Colorado Spruce. Leaves radially spreading, to 1¼ inches long, and when plants are raised from seed variable in color from nearly green to pale blue-gray. The better-known varieties are vegetatively propagated, however, and therefore reasonably uniform in their blue-gray or silvery color. Shoots stout, orange-brown, without hairs. Cones with a reddish tinge, to 4 inches long.

Some of the better-known varieties of *P. pungens* are: *Kosteriana*, Koster Blue Spruce, a tree of narrow outline with pendulous branches and foliage of a bluish-silvery color and the most popular of all the varieties. The height of many homeowners' ambition seems to be to own one, or a pair, of this plant without any regard to its appropriateness to the surroundings in which it is to be planted, with the result that it is much over-planted. Where it has a background of dark foliage it is a very striking plant but in the most suitable surroundings should be used sparingly. It is not suitable for every suburban front yard, as its light color is much too pronounced. Var. *glauca* has more silvery leaves than the previous variety, and var. *Moerheimii* is another with silvery foliage but is broader in habit than Koster Blue Spruce, and the branches are horizontal. There are a few bushy forms, none of them so well known as the foregoing, of which var. *compacta* is probably the commonest.

Picea rubens, "RED SPRUCE." Northeastern United States and Canada. Like the Black Spruce, with which it is often confused, this one dislikes a low elevation and warm climate and is not a good garden tree. Leaves bright green, shiny, crowded, to ¾ inch long. Shoots brown, very short-hairy. Cones green or purplish, to 1½ inches long.

Besides those mentioned here, there are several other kinds of Spruce in cultivation which are omitted either because they are unsatisfactory for garden use or because they are uncommon.

PINACEAE

PINUS, "PINE." Some of the larger Pines are among the stateliest of evergreen trees when they are growing in positions allowing for their full development. Some, like the Eastern White Pine, *P. Strobus*, grow quite rapidly, while others are of much slower growth and for many years can be grown in rather restricted surroundings.

Pines require a soil adequately drained, and the majority of them are suitable for the drier, sandier types of soil that are unsuited to Fir or Spruce. Their branches arise in whorls or tiers around the trunk as in those trees, but the whorls are usually much better defined.

Pine leaves are not spaced singly along the shoots, but occur in bundles normally of two, three, or five leaves. The Pines with five leaves in each bundle are distinguished as Soft or White Pines, and when their wood has economic value it is soft, white, and not very resinous. Those Pines with two or three leaves to a bundle are known, with a few exceptions, as Pitch or Hard Pines, and those members of this group that are of economic value for their wood usually have a harder, yellower, more resinous wood.

The leaves of Pines are rounded on the undersides, and are either flat on the upper, as is the case of those with two leaves to a bundle, or have two upper surfaces when there are three or five leaves to a bundle. There are minute teeth on the leaf margins of most Pines, and the seeds of a few species are edible.

In the following pages the Pines are divided into three groups according to the number of leaves to a bundle, and so are in alphabetical order only within each group.

The following Pines have five leaves to a bundle:

Pinus aristata, "BRISTLECONE PINE," "HICKORY PINE." A slow-growing tree, or in the East usually a shrub about as broad as tall, generally comparatively small, and not common. It is peculiar for the numerous little specks of resin which dot its leaves and which, on superficial observation, might well be mistaken for scale insects. Leaves without marginal teeth, stiff, dark green, to 1½ inches long. Shoots glabrous, or at first sparingly short-hairy. Cones to 3½ inches long. Western United States.

This tree has recently come into prominence through its claim to being the oldest living thing in the world, tree-ring counts having shown several trees in California to be over 4000 years old. It thereby displaces the tree which had previously held this distinction, namely the Giant Sequoia, *Sequoiadendron giganteum*, of California, some of which are said to be more than 3000 years old.

Pinus Armandii. China, Formosa. In many respects this Pine is similar to *P. nepalensis*. Leaves slender, often drooping, to 6 inches long, and usually with a distinct kink near the base. Winter buds slightly resinous. Shoots greenish, without hairs, but often glandular, and not glaucous as in *P. nepalensis*. Cones to 7 inches long.

Pinus Cembra, "SWISS STONE PINE." A very ornamental and desirable Pine of slow, dense growth which for many years is rather narrowly pyramidal in outline. Leaves to 4 inches long, pointing forward, the clusters closely set on the shoot. Winter buds resinous. Shoots thickly covered with short, brown hairs. Cones to 3 inches long. Central Europe to Asia.

Pinus flexilis, "LIMBER PINE." Western North America. Compared to most other Pines this one, when young, sometimes appears rather thin in habit, as the leaves are crowded toward the ends of the shoots, but with increasing age it is of considerable ornamental value. Leaves without teeth, slender, to 3 inches long. Shoots minutely hairy. Cones to 6 inches long.

Pinus koraiensis, "KOREAN PINE." Japan and Korea. Of similar appearance to the Swiss Stone Pine but usually with rather grayer, longer leaves, to 4½ inches, which spread more than in the latter, and the plant of rather wider outline, and a little faster growth, but equally pleasing in appearance. Shoots covered with very short, brownish hairs. Cones to 5 inches long.

Pinus Lambertiana, "SUGAR PINE." Western United States. In the Northeast this Pine should be grown only in positions protected from the coldest winds, and it grows slowly. In its native stands it is remarkable for the immense size of its

Pinus Cembra, "SWISS STONE PINE"

cones, which may sometimes be as much as 20 inches long. It is the most massive of all the Pines when in its natural habitat, has an open manner of branching and usually rather short, pendulous branches. Leaves to 4 inches long, rigid and thick. Shoots brown, and fine-hairy.

Pinus monticola, "MOUNTAIN WHITE PINE." Western North America. Generally similar to the Eastern White Pine *P. Strobus,* but narrower in outline, and with rather shorter, stouter leaves to 4 inches long. Shoots covered with reddish down. Cones narrow, to 8 inches long, occasionally longer.

Pinus nepalensis (P. excelsa). "HIMALAYAN PINE." Himalayas to Afghanistan. A large, widely branched, fast-growing, very handsome Pine, but somewhat dejected-looking in winter because of its markedly drooping leaves. Leaves gray-green, slender, often with a bend near the base, to 7 inches long. Shoots covered with a blue-gray bloom but without hairs. Cones narrow, to 10 inches long.

Pinus parviflora, "JAPANESE WHITE PINE." It seems probable that the only form of this tree grown here is one cultivated in Japanese gardens, rather than the wild plant. It is of peculiar habit, with 2- to 3-inch, thin, twisted, grayish leaves which occur in bunches at the ends of the shoots. An interesting small tree of rather slow, very irregular growth, often as broad at the base as it is tall, and usually odd-looking because of its uneven branching and the peculiar way in which the leaves are clustered at the ends of the shoots. It produces cones when quite small, and these hang on the tree for several years; opinions vary about their ornamental quality after they have turned black with age.

Pinus Peuce, "MACEDONIAN PINE." Another of the very ornamental Pines of narrow outline and slow growth, similar to that of *P. Cembra.* Leaves to 4 inches long, the bundles closely spaced on the shoots. Shoots green and without hairs, although these are present in *P. Cembra* and *P. koraiensis*. Cones to 5 inches long. Balkans.

Pinus Strobus, "EASTERN WHITE PINE." This native of eastern North America is a particularly handsome representative of the White Pines, and can usually be counted on to make a good showing in the Northeast. Unfortunately, it makes too large a tree for the small property, but where space is available its large size and soft, grayish foliage can be a very satisfying feature of the landscape. Leaves to 5 inches long, slender, soft, grayish. Shoots at first minutely downy, soon smooth. Cones to 6 or occasionally to 10 inches long. In addition to some not very common dwarf forms, one other, but also uncommon, is worth noting. This is var. *fastigiata*, a tall, narrowly upright tree suitable for many positions where the parent species would be too broad.

The following Pines have two leaves to each bundle:

Pinus Banksiana, "JACK PINE." A northern North American Pine, generally small and with crooked branches, and little regarded as a garden tree though extremely hardy and useful for planting on dry, sandy soils subject to wind erosion. Leaves stiff, curved, and twisted, to 1½ inches long. Shoots yellowish, devoid of hairs. Winter buds resinous. Cones to 2 inches long, curved at the end, and remaining on the branches for many years.

Pinus contorta, "SHORE PINE." Another small tree, but from California and other western states and doubtfully hardy north of Virginia. Sometimes grown in the East is its var. *latifolia*, Lodgepole Pine, which is hardier and taller. This is the inland, mountain form, and has rather longer, twisted, stiff leaves to 3 inches long and very resinous winter buds.

Pinus densiflora, "JAPANESE RED PINE." This is one of the Pines commonly grown in small, ornamental containers by the Japanese and, by skillful training and pruning in order to dwarf them, made to look like gnarled old trees taken from positions of extreme exposure to the elements. After its early years it is not usually one of the most handsome as a garden tree, though the stem sometimes develops picturesque curves. Leaves rather light green, slender, to 4½ inches long. Winter buds slightly resinous. Shoots with a glaucous bloom. Cones to 2 inches long. A variety, *umbraculifera,* is a much more popular garden plant, and goes by the name Tanyosho Pine. This does not form a single stem but is densely branched with branches that curve upward, and is broader at the top than the base. In time it becomes a very large shrub, often with a flattish top. It is sometimes used in foundation plantings but, unless there is a very large wall space to cover, almost inevitably becomes too big.

Pinus echinata, "short-leaf pine." Although a valuable native timber tree this Pine does not find much use in gardens. Not infrequently there are three or four slender, slightly twisted leaves up to 4 inches long to the clusters. Shoots usually flushed violet, and with a glaucous bloom. Cones to 2½ inches long. Southern New York to Florida and inland.

Pinus Mugo (P. montana), "mountain pine." A Pine of the mountains of central and southern Europe, but divided into varieties according to certain minor botanical characters, principally of the cones, and its geographical distribution. Some of these varieties are small trees, while others are tall or low, densely branched shrubs. For garden purposes the more dwarfed, shrubby forms, usually represented by the var. *Mughus,* are the more popular, and in addition to their value in border and foundation plantings are excellent for covering banks and can be grown on limestone soils. Leaves of var. *Mughus* to 3 inches long, dark green, curved, the clusters thickly set on the shoots. Winter buds resinous. Shoots greenish brown, without hairs. Cones to 2½ inches long.

Pinus nigra (*P. austriaca, P. Laricio*), "AUSTRIAN PINE." This Pine has a wide distribution in central and southern Europe and Asia Minor, but according to its geographical location, and to differences in length of leaf and size of cone, it is divided into a number of varieties, but with the exception of the Austrian Pine they are not very commonly grown in this country.

The Austrian Pine grows well, and is a handsome tree quite common in gardens. It is tolerant of city conditions, but not then seen at its best; equally good near the sea, it will tolerate a certain amount of salt spray, and it is also useful for windbreaks or shelter belts. Leaves very dark green, stiff, to 4 inches long. Shoots light brown, without hairs. Winter buds brown, resinous. Cones to 3 inches long. There are several dwarf forms of this Pine.

Pinus pungens, "POVERTY PINE." This native of eastern states, from New Jersey southward, is not sufficiently ornamental for garden use, as it is too open and irregular in habit. Leaves, sometimes three to a cluster, dark green, stiff, twisted, and curved, to 3 inches long. Shoots yellow-brown, devoid of hairs. Cones to 3 inches long.

Pinus resinosa, "RED PINE." Another eastern American species with long, soft leaves, commonly grown in gardens. Unfortunately, it is very subject to attack by the European pine-shoot moth, which will ruin it in a very few years unless systematic control is employed. It is also very intolerant of shade. Leaves thin and flexible, to 6 inches long. Winter buds resinous. Shoots yellow-brown, without hairs. Cones to 2¼ inches long.

Pinus sylvestris, "SCOTS PINE." This Pine has been extensively planted in America, not only as a garden tree, but to some extent in reforestation. As its common name suggests, it

Pinus resinosa, "RED PINE"

is a European species, and is widely distributed across that continent to Siberia; different forms of it are recognized according to their geographical location, but are of no concern here. The Scots Pine is usually readily distinguished by its definitely gray-green, stiff, twisted leaves, to 2¾ inches long. Winter buds resinous. Shoots light green, without hairs, and cones to 2½ inches long. Old trees have very beautiful trunks of a rich red-brown.

Pinus Thunbergii, "JAPANESE BLACK PINE." This Pine is very similar in appearance to the Austrian Pine, but may usually be distinguished from it by its almost white, nonresinous winter buds, as compared to the brown, resinous buds of the latter. The Japanese Black Pine has proved to be the best of all the Pines for planting near the sea in the Northeast, as salt spray seems to have very little, if any, injurious effect upon it. Also, it is another of the Pines grown and dwarfed in ornamental containers by the Japanese. Leaves dark green, stiff, to 4½ inches long. Shoots orange, without hairs, and cones to 2¼ inches long.

Pinus virginiana, "SCRUB PINE." This Pine of the eastern states, which may be tree-like or shrubby, is of little value in the garden, but like the Jack Pine is useful for planting on poor, worn-out soils, though it lacks the extreme hardiness of the latter. Leaves usually twisted and curved, to 3 inches long. Shoots purplish, glaucous. Cones to 2½ inches long.

The following Pines have three leaves to each bundle:

Pinus Bungeana, "LACE-BARK PINE." A small, rather slow-growing tree, or as it most frequently produces more than one stem from the base, often thinly bushy rather than tree-like. Its most interesting characteristic is the manner in which patches of bark flake off the stems in the same manner as in the deciduous Button-ball tree, exposing the pale yellowish green new bark beneath, which is in sharp contrast to the older, darker bark

128

Pyracantha coccinea Lalandii, "LALAND FIRETHORN"

Rhododendron hybrid, ALBUM GRANDIFLORUM

still adhering to the stems. Leaves light green, stiff, to 3 inches long, the leaf bundles rather thinly spaced on the shoots. Shoots gray-green, without hairs. Cones to 2½ inches long.

Pinus cembroides, "MEXICAN STONE PINE." From some southwestern states and Mexico, this plant is very doubtfully hardy north of Washington, D.C., but two of its varieties are hardier, and one of them occasionally is to be found in northeastern gardens. This one is the interesting var. *monophylla,* which should have only one leaf in place of the customary two, three, or five common to the leaf bundles of most Pines. But this feature of a single leaf is not completely uniform, and not infrequently there are two leaves. The plant grows slowly and usually is a bush of rather small size. Leaves without marginal teeth, to 1½ inches long, stiff, glaucous-green, and with a hard point. Shoots gray-brown, without hairs. Cones to 2 inches long.

Pinus Coulteri, "COULTER'S PINE." This Californian Pine is better adapted to areas south of Washington, D.C., though it is occasionally found in gardens further north. It is a tree of open habit with the leaves crowded at the ends of the shoots. Leaves dark green or occasionally bluish green, stiff, drooping, to 12 inches long. Winter buds resinous. Shoots stout, with a glaucous bloom. Cones to 12 or more inches long.

Pinus Jeffreyi, "JEFFREY'S PINE." From Oregon and California, this tree has a narrow outline, and rather open branching. Leaves distinctly blue-green, stiff, to 10 inches long. *P. Jeffreyi* is very similar to *P. ponderosa,* but differs in its bluish foliage, bloomy shoots, and nonresinous buds. Cones to 10 inches long.

Pinus ponderosa, "WESTERN YELLOW PINE." One of the most important timber trees of this country, covering immense tracts in the West. A tree of narrow outline, with short, often drooping branches. Sometimes the leaf clusters may contain two, four, or five leaves rather than the more normal three. Leaves stiff, curved, drooping, to 10 inches long. Winter buds resinous. Shoots reddish brown or greenish, without hairs. Cones to 7 inches long.

Pinus rigida, "PITCH PINE." Another eastern Pine, but not one of the more ornamental as a garden tree, as it is apt to be very irregular in habit; however, it is another of those of value for holding poor sandy soils. It is peculiar for the manner in which very short, leaf-bearing shoots arise on the trunk and older portions of the branches, often in great numbers. Leaves dark green, stiff, twisted, to 4½ inches long. Shoots pale brown, ridged, without hairs. Cones to 2½ inches long, often two or more together, which remain on the branches for many years and frequently occur on the trunk.

Pinus Taeda, "LOBLOLLY PINE." Native to southern Atlantic states and inland, and though of importance as a timber tree its ornamental value is small and it is not sufficiently hardy much north of New Jersey. Leaves slender, but firm, slightly twisted, light green, to 9 inches long. Not infrequently there are two rather than three leaves to a bundle. Shoots greenish brown, without hairs, and cones to 4½ inches long.

PINACEAE

PSEUDOTSUGA. Of the very few species of this genus only one, *P. mucronata,* Douglas Fir, has assumed any importance as an ornamental. The Pseudotsugas take a position somewhere between the Firs and the Spruces, having some characters common to both. The leaves are flattened as in Fir, and when they fall from the shoots the latter are left nearly as smooth to the touch as in Fir, whereas in Spruce they are rough with the persistent leaf bases. The cones are pendulous in *Pseudotsuga*, and the whole cone falls when mature as it does in Spruce. But *Pseudotsuga* cones have another distinction—very prominent three-lobed bracts project from between the cone scales, the center lobe being the longest and narrowest. Bracts also project from some Fir cones, but they are not three-lobed. Probably the simplest means of distinguishing *Pseudotsuga* from Fir and Spruce is by examining the winter buds, which are quite long, drawn out to a point, and not resinous. The branches of *Pseudotsuga* are not arranged in such regular whorls as in Fir and Spruce, but arise at more irregular intervals on the trunk.

Pseudotsuga mucronata (*P. Douglasii, P. taxifolia*), "DOUG-LAS FIR." This tree comes from northwestern America, where it is of great importance for its timber. There are, however, coastal and mountain forms of it, the coastal form, distinguished as var. *viridis*, has green foliage, and the mountain form, var. *glauca*, has blue-gray foliage. The coastal form is not always sufficiently hardy for the northeastern region, but the mountain form does well and is the one now most frequently used in eastern gardens, and it makes a handsome tree. Leaves of the mountain form usually bluish-gray, though in some plants they are nearly green, ¾–1 inch long, with two grayish bands beneath, blunt-ended. Shoots yellow-green and short-hairy. Winter buds long-pointed, without resin. Cones to 2 inches long, with exserted three-lobed bracts between the cone scales.

PINACEAE

Retinispora or *Retinospora*. A synonym of some of the *Chamaecyparis*, but principally for juvenile forms of *C. obtusa* and *C. pisifera*.

SCIADOPITYS. The species given below is the only one in the genus.

Sciadopitys verticillata, "UMBRELLA PINE." This very ornamental native of Japan stands out among other conifers for the manner in which its long leaves radiate around the top of the year's shoots, suggesting the ribs of an umbrella. There have been differences of opinion among botanists as to which were the true leaves, though modern theory generally holds to the belief that each so-called leaf is actually two leaves joined together along one edge. Another, older theory held that the small scales which occur on the otherwise naked lower portion of the shoots were the true leaves, and the organs now commonly regarded as leaves were shoots or cladodes, that is, green stems serving the function of leaves.

The Umbrella Pine varies in habit; sometimes it is quite bushy, developing a number of stems from near the base of the main one so that it forms a broad-based pyramid for many years, while other plants quickly show a tree-like habit with dominant trunk and shorter lateral branches. In either case the plant does not grow rapidly and, though after its early years it is usually hardy, it is advisable to plant it in positions protected from cold winds.

Leaves to 5 inches long, very shiny, with a longitudinal groove on both surfaces, with two white bands beneath, and notched at the end. Cones to 4 inches long.

SEQUOIA. The genus contains only one species, but see also *Sequoiadendron.*

Sciadopitys verticillata, "UMBRELLA PINE"

Sequoia sempervirens, "REDWOOD." The Redwood is included here only as a matter of interest, as it is not sufficiently hardy for growing in the East, its natural home being in the fog belt of California and lower Oregon. But it is the tallest and among the most noteworthy trees of the world, sometimes growing to a height of well over 300 feet, with a trunk diameter to 25 feet or occasionally more. It is noteworthy for another reason, being one of the few conifers that will sprout and regenerate from cut or fallen stumps. Some years ago Redwood "burls" were quite common in florists' shops, and when placed in water they sprouted minature forests of shoots.

PINACEAE

SEQUOIADENDRON. Contains the one species given here. Until quite recently this tree and the previous one, *Sequoia,* were both included in the genus *Sequioa;* now, however, they are treated as belonging to separate genera.

Sequoiadendron giganteum (*Sequoia gigantea, S. Wellingtonia, Wellingtonia gigantea*), "GIANT SEQUOIA," "BIGTREE." The Giant Sequoias are the most massive, and for many years have been believed to be the oldest, living things in the world. The latter distinction, however, has recently been claimed for the much smaller Bristlecone Pine *Pinus aristata,* when growing in areas of little rainfall and extreme exposure, the very opposite natural conditions to those enjoyed by the Giant Sequoias.

The Giant Sequoias are now native to a limited area of California, though the fossil remains of this or similar trees have been turned up in many widely separated places, indicating that at one time they had a wide distribution in the world. The "General Sherman Bigtree" is famous, having a trunk diameter of thirty-five feet, and an estimated age of more than 2500 years, though the age of others has been placed at well above 3000 years.

Sequoiadendron does not take kindly to the East, preferring a more equable climate, but where a collection of trees is being grown it is not uncommon to find young trees of it. The very severe winters experienced in the East at widely separated intervals frequently mean the death of any but those specimens growing in the most favorable locations, but they are interesting as long as they last.

Leaves scale-like, hardly ¼ inch long, parallel with and usually rather closely pressed to the shoots for the greater part of their length, but the tips free. It seems a little strange that so massive a tree should have cones only 2–3 inches long.

TAXACEAE

TAXUS, "YEW." Few evergreen shrubs are so popular in gardens as the Yews, and this popularity has increased enormously within the past thirty years or so with the increased propagation of clonal forms and some hybrids. For northeastern gardens the Japanese Yew, *T. cuspidata,* and its varieties have outstripped in favor the only other widely cultivated species, namely the English Yew, *T. baccata,* and its varieties. To some, the very dark green foliage of the Yews is not pleasing, but they have the advantage of being very shade tolerant and of all conifers the best for city conditions.

There is still some uncertainty about the poisonous effect of Yew foliage on livestock when they browse on it, though there is no doubt that deaths to stock have occurred as a result. But it is equally certain that there are other instances where no harm has followed. There can be little question, however, about the poisonous effect of wilted Yew foliage, and there are many well-authenticated cases of fatal results where cattle have eaten cut branches that had wilted after they were cast aside. The seeds also are poisonous, and children should be warned not to eat them, but the red aril or coat which partly encloses the seed is harmless.

The leaves of Yews, though arising spirally on the shoots, are arranged in two opposite ranks, and have two much paler bands on the underside. The sexes normally occur on separate plants, only rarely on the same plant, and the flowers of both are negligible. The fleshy, red arils which partly enclose the seeds are very showy when there is a large seed crop.

Taxus baccata, "ENGLISH YEW." Occurring wild over parts of Europe, North Africa, and western Asia, this plant has been cultivated in Europe for many centuries. It plays an important part in English folklore, and before the days of gunpowder its boughs were highly valued for making archers' bows. There are trees in Britain said to be from 800 to well over 1000 years old. It is not quite so well adapted to the American climate as the Japanese Yew, *T. cuspidata*, as it is not so hardy, though on the older estates it is not unusual to find good specimens of some of its seemingly hardier varieties. It is not readily distinguished from its Japanese counterpart, but on horizontal shoots its leaves as a rule do not form a channel on the upper side, but spread more flatly and are gradually drawn out to a point, whereas in the latter they are more abruptly pointed. They are 1–1¼ inches in length, with two pale green bands beneath. The shoots remain green the second year.

A great many varieties are recognized in Europe, but a much smaller number are to be found in American nurseries. Var. *adpressa* makes a dense, slowly spreading bush, and has very short, crowded leaves about ½ inch long. Another form of it,

Taxus baccata stricta, "IRISH YEW"

adpressa stricta, has stiffly upright shoots. Var. *aurea* is a golden-foliaged bush form remarkable for the bright color of its new foliage, which, however, turns green as the season advances. This form may be raised from seed, but seedling plants differ considerably in the degree of golden color, and those of outstanding color should be vegetatively propagated. Var. *Dovastonii,* Westfelton Yew, assumes tree size, with a trunk, horizontal branches, and long, pendulous shoots. Var. *lutea* has yellow arils surrounding the seeds. Var. *repandens* is probably the hardiest form of the English Yew and quite common in gardens. It is a low, flat, wide-spreading plant with drooping branches and often with curved leaves. Var. *stricta* (var. *fastigiata* or *T. hibernica*), Irish Yew. A very attractive plant with crowded upright branches, with the leaves radiating around the shoots, not in two ranks. Eventually this plant grows into a broad, parallel-sided, short column. Unfortunately, it is not entirely hardy, and plants that are severely injured, as in the winter of 1933–34, take a considerable time to recover. There are many other varieties, some with variegated foliage.

Taxus brevifolia, "WESTERN YEW." Native to northwestern America, and rare in the East as it is not sufficiently hardy. It is not to be confused with a variety of *T. cuspidata* often incorrectly catalogued as var. *brevifolia* but sometimes merely as *T. brevifolia.*

Taxus canadensis, "CANADA YEW." This is another native, but of eastern North America, of considerably less ornamental value than the English or Japanese Yews, but because of its shade preference sometimes grown as an underplanting among trees. A loose, straggling plant which, particularly when exposed to winter sun, assumes an unpleasant brownish color. Usually quite low and spreading, though it may grow to a height of about 4 feet. Leaves to ¾ inch long, narrow, with two pale bands beneath, ending in a short point. A more attractive form of it with upright shoots is var. *stricta,* which will reach a height of 2 feet or a little more. It can be grown as a low hedge and is also a suitable rock garden shrub.

Taxus cuspidata, "JAPANESE YEW." One of the best Yews for eastern gardens, as it is hardy and pleasing in appearance, and in the varieties is obtainable in different shapes. Leaves about 1 inch long, ending in a rather abrupt point, with two paler bands beneath. On horizontal shoots the leaves on the two sides commonly form a rather narrow V-shaped channel, and the two-year-old branches are usually reddish brown. Of its varieties, that known as *capitata* is the upright form and is raised from seed, though there are wide variations in habit of growth among seedling plants, and it develops into a broad-based pyramid with a central stem—often more than one if the extra ones are not removed—and forward-pointing branches. A favorite for foundation plantings, but in time may become too large. Var. *densa* is slow-growing, and though usually broader than high is a nicely rounded plant. Var. *nana,* often incorrectly called *brevifolia,* grows much more rapidly than the latter, and is a wide-spreading shrub much broader than high. It is generally too vigorous for foundation plantings, though much used for that purpose, but develops into a handsome plant where it has ample room to spread. Var. *Thayerae* makes a taller, broad shrub with somewhat ascending branches. There are other lesser known varieties.

Taxus Hunnewelliana. This is believed to be a hybrid between *T. cuspidata* and *canadensis,* is a rather loosely branched but graceful shrub with upward curving branches, and seems to show the influence of its *T. canadensis* parent in its brownish winter foliage.

Taxus media. This is also a hybrid, with *T. baccata* and *T. cuspidata* as its parents, and there are a number of forms that are becoming very popular in gardens. They seem to have a degree of hardiness at least equal to that of *T. cuspidata,* and the leaves most nearly resemble that species, though in their more regular two-ranked and frequently horizontal arrangement on the shoots they favor *T. baccata.* Var. *Andersonii* is a broad, bushy plant; var. *Brownii* tends to be about as broad as it is tall, but grows rather slowly. Var. *Hatfieldii* is broadly conical in outline, and dense with upright shoots clothed with radially spreading leaves. Var. *Hicksii* is more columnar in form, though not infrequently broader at the top than the base, unless this tendency is restricted by pruning. Var. *Kelseyi* is taller than broad, and a free-fruiting form. Several other varieties are in cultivation, but as many of them are comparatively new their ultimate form will become apparent as they attain greater size.

PINACEAE

THUJA (THUYA), "ARBORVITAE." The Arborvitaes are one of the most useful groups of coniferous shrubs, more particularly the varieties of two species, one native to eastern North America and the other to Asia. The leaves of the Arborvitaes are small and scale-like, more or less closely pressed to the shoots except in a few varieties with juvenile leaves, then they are awl-shaped and stand away from the shoots. Flowers and cones of no ornamental value.

Thuja koraiensis, "KOREAN ARBORVITAE." Little known as a garden plant and of only botanical interest. Usually a low shrub, rarely a small tree, with spreading upturned branches, the leaves of which are very grayish white beneath.

Thuja occidentalis, "AMERICAN ARBORVITAE." This native of the eastern states and Canada is a plant of moist, often swampy ground, and should not be planted in very dry soils. It is commonly used as a garden plant, and is very useful for hedges, its upright, densely branched habit making it a good subject for this purpose. Some of its numerous varieties, however, are in much greater demand as ornamentals, and the extreme hardiness of most of them has undoubtedly contributed to their popularity. However, those characters which in the young plants of some varieties serve to distinguish them often become indefinite with age and greatly increased size, and at that stage positive identification of the variety frequently is impossible. The terminal growth on the shoots is generally in more or less horizontal planes. Unfortunately, the foliage often assumes a brownish tinge in winter which is not so pleasing as the green of some other conifers, but this is discounted by its other good qualities. Some of the more popular varieties follow: *compacta* is a dense, rather slow-growing pyramidal form; var. *Douglasii pyramidalis* is a most attractive pyramidal plant with the ends of the shoots crested or fern-like; var. *Ellwangeriana* is a broadly rounded shrub with mixed juvenile and adult foliage that becomes brownish in winter, and unless the plant is occasionally pruned or sheared is apt to become floppy as it attains size. Its golden-foliaged form, *Ellwangeriana aurea* is not particularly ornamental. Var. *ericoides* is of much slower growth than *Ellwangeriana* and with entirely juvenile foliage of a light, bright green color in summer which becomes a pleasing purple with the approach of cold weather. Var. *fastigiata* is a narrow columnar form useful as an accent plant or for a tall, narrow hedge. Var. *globosa* is spherical in outline and better adapted to use in positions requiring a somewhat formal shape than to a mixed border. Var. *Hoveyi* is ovate in outline and a light shade of green; var. *Ohlendorfii,* a slow-growing form in which the two kinds of foliage, adult and juvenile, are at all times very well distinguished. It turns quite brown in the fall of the year, but in common with other varieties regains its green color in spring. Var. *pumila*, Little Gem, is a very low, slowly spreading plant for use in the front of borders or foundation plantings. Var. *robusta* (var. *sibirica*, var. *Wareana*), is a broadly pyramidal plant, with foliage of good dark color which changes little in winter, and dense habit; var. *Rosenthalii* is another of very good color, but of more rapid growth than var. *robusta* and more columnar in shape. Var. *umbraculifera*, a rather low, broad-topped, vase-shaped bush; and var. *Woodwardii* is a spherical form that holds its green color well in winter.

There are also several colored and variegated forms of which the following may be mentioned: var. Columbia is probably the best of the silver-variegated forms, as the white shoot tips are quite pronounced in winter. Var. *lutea*, George Peabody Golden, is the best of the golden-foliaged forms, with the ends of the shoots brightly colored. Var. *Douglasii aurea* is another with good pyramidal form and pleasing color. There are many other varieties in cultivation.

Thuja orientalis (*Biota orientalis*), "ORIENTAL ARBOR-VITAE." China and Korea. This tree is not hardy over so wide an area as *T. occidentalis*, though by no means uncommon in the wide suburban surroundings of New York City. It is much more frequently represented, however, by some of its varieties, most of which are probably more tender than the parent species but find great favor in the more southerly states. The Oriental Arborvitae is quite handsome as a small tree, and is noteworthy for the manner in which the branches and their branchlets, equally green on both sides, form flat, vertical plates, but as they are closely pressed together this feature is not obvious at a distance. Unfortunately, as it increases in size the branches sometimes begin to fall apart, and, unless they are tied in, the plant begins to look untidy. Many of its varieties are very ornamental and of a much brighter green than those of the American Arborvitae, but in northern areas are prone to "burning" on the sunny side in winter.

Among the better-known varieties are *aurea* (*aurea nana*), Berckman's Golden Arborvitae, the most popular of the many varietal forms of this tree. It is broadly pyramidal and has bright golden young foliage which later changes to light green. Var. *bonita* is more ovate in shape, but does not have quite such pronounced color in its spring foliage. Var. *conspicua* is densely fastigiate, with the golden spring foliage interfused with green; var. *decussata* is a broadly pyramidal plant with entirely juvenile foliage of a bluish green; var. *elegantissima* is rather stiffly columnar, of slow growth, with yellow spring foliage which becomes light green later. Var. *rosedalis* usually grows quite slowly, and the foliage is entirely juvenile with interesting changes from the spring green to gray-green to bronzy purple in winter. It is apt to suffer damage on the sunny side in winter. Var. *Sieboldii* (*compacta*) is a rounded shrub with light green foliage the year around. Var. *stricta* (*pyramidalis*) is dense, broadly pyramidal, and green the year around.

Thuja plicata (*T. gigantea, T. Lobbii*), "GIANT ARBOR- VITAE." This Arborvitae grows rapidly into a tall, very hand- some pyramidal tree. Coming from western North America, in the Northeast it should be planted in positions where it has protection from the coldest winds. The shiny leaves are rather larger than those of any other species, with silvery markings on the underside. Var. *atrovirens* has foliage of a darker green, and does not grow quite so rapidly. Var. *fastigiata* is much narrower in outline than the parent species.

Thuja Standishii, "JAPANESE ARBORVITAE." A broadly pyramidal tree with spreading branches, of rather slow growth, the foliage bright green with white markings beneath. It is not common in cultivation but appears to be quite hardy.

THUJOPSIS. Contains the one species given here.

Thujopsis dolabrata (*Thuja dolabrata*), "HIBA ARBOR-VITAE." *Thujopsis* is distinguished from *Thuja* by characters not readily detected except by the botanist. Its leaves are rather larger, and broader in proportion to their length, than in any *Thuja,* and the branchlets are much flattened. It originates in Japan and is not among the hardiest conifers, and it is doubtful whether it attains the proportions of a tree in the Northeast, as the few specimens encountered are usually shrubs.

TAXACEAE

TORREYA. Though small trees in their native surroundings, the Torreyas are more likely to be shrubby in cultivation, and with the exception of *T. nucifera* are not reliably hardy in the Northeast. Their general appearance strongly suggests Yews.

Torreya californica, "CALIFORNIA NUTMEG," originates in that state and is sometimes grown in a sheltered position in the Northeast, but is better adapted to Washington, D.C., and south. Leaves to 2½ inches long, dark green and shiny above, drawn out to a spiny point, and with two grayish, narrow, sunken bands beneath.

Torreya grandis. China. Probably a little hardier than *T. californica,* but uncommon. Leaves to 1 inch long, thinner and paler green than in *T. nucifera,* and the two-year-old shoots green, whereas in *T. californica* and *T. nucifera* they are reddish or brown.

Torreya nucifera. This Japanese plant will grow into a large, handsome, pyramidal shrub or small tree. Leaves to 1¼ inches long, dark green above, ending in a spiny point, with two sunken bands beneath. The plum-like fruits are about 1 inch long, practically stalkless, green or purple tinged, and ripen in their second year.

Torreya taxifolia is native to Florida and adapted only to the extreme South and Gulf States.

PINACEAE

TSUGA "HEMLOCK." Graceful trees with small leaves and pliant, horizontal branches that sway with every breeze. The Hemlock in greatest use in the East is Common Hemlock, *T. canadensis,* but some other species are more ornamental. Hemlocks require a moist soil, preferably one containing an adequate amount of organic matter, and though in nature they are found on quite steep hillsides, in the East now most frequently in mixture with hardwoods, the soil surface in such places is protected by a layer of decaying vegetable matter which preserves the soil moisture. Hemlocks should not be planted where they are exposed to the coldest winds, a condition unfavorable to all of them and often causing some defoliation. Leaves usually arranged in two opposite ranks along the shoots, though they arise spirally around them, and they are flattened, much in the manner of many Firs, but thinner. The branches, however, do not grow in regular whorls or tiers around the main stem, but arise irregularly. The cones are rather small, in most species to about 1 inch long, and they hang down on the shoots.

Tsuga canadensis, "COMMON HEMLOCK." Native to

eastern North America and quite hardy, this plant is of value in the garden in groups, and as isolated specimens, and in foundation plantings, and for hedges. It is quite shade tolerant, but when grown where there is much shade the foliage is not so dense as when it has better exposure. Quite commonly it produces more than one stem from the base, and unless all except the main one are suppressed it becomes bushy. Leaves to ⅔ inch long, with fine teeth on the margins and two narrow whitish bands beneath, and usually blunt-pointed. Shoots finely downy. A number of varieties are recognized, but few of them are available in nurseries. Some of these are trees differing in habit of growth and size of leaves, and others are shrubs of various shapes. Quite well known and readily procured is the variety *pendula* (*Sargentii pendula*), a plant broader than high, with drooping branches and a flattish top. Eventually, but slowly, this will become a very large mound of foliage, green to the ground and many feet in diameter. It is of interest to note that the original four seedlings of this popular variety were found growing wild near Fishkill, New York.

Tsuga caroliniana, "CAROLINA HEMLOCK." From the mountains of Virginia and Georgia, this is a handsomer plant than *T. canadensis*, and it is unfortunate that it is not more often substituted for the latter. It does not grow quite so rapidly, and the branches do not spread so widely as those of *T. canadensis* but commonly assume a more drooping habit, and the foliage is denser. Leaves to ¾ inch long, with two well-defined white bands beneath but without teeth on their margins, rounded or notched at the tip. Shoots slightly downy in the grooves.

Tsuga diversifolia, "JAPANESE HEMLOCK." This is another very ornamental tree, distinctly pyramidal rather than rounded in form as *T. canadensis* often is, but of slower growth.

146

Leaves about ½ inch long, notched at the tip, without teeth, with two narrow white bands beneath. Shoots downy.

Tsuga heterophylla, "western hemlock." From the Northwest, and as it requires a moist climate is not often satisfactory in the East and not sufficiently hardy. It is a distinctly pyramidal tree. Leaves about ½ inch long, with finely toothed margins, with two broad grayish bands beneath, and rounded at the tip. Shoots with long whitish hairs.

Tsuga Mertensiana, "mountain hemlock." Originating in the same general region as *T. heterophylla,* this one suffers similar disabilities in the East, but is a little the better of the two. Leaves to ¾ inch long, radiating around the shoots, not in two ranks, finely toothed and blunt-pointed, with stomatic lines on both surfaces, which give the foliage a grayish appearance. Shoots downy. Cones to 2½ inches long.

Tsuga Sieboldii. Another interesting Japanese species, but in cultivation this one is usually more shrubby in habit than tree-like, as its tendency is to produce several stems from the base. Leaves to ¾ inch long, without teeth, usually broadest and notched at tip, with two narrow white bands beneath. Shoots without down.

7 The Broad-leaved Evergreens

The term "broad-leaved evergreens" is used to denote those evergreens with woody stems that are not conifers, the latter, as was explained in Chapter 1, being known as "narrow-leaved evergreens." It must be noted, however, that the use of the word "broad-leaved" is relative and may be misleading to those unfamiliar with the two terms, as a few of the plants it contains have leaves as narrow as in some conifers, which are far from uniform in width though generally much narrower in proportion to their length than is the case with the majority of the broad-leaved group.

The plants of the Heath family are also a part of the broad-leaved group, and are given in Chapter 8, and the reasons for their exclusion from this chapter are given there.

In order to give a general picture of the broad-leaved evergreens, a number of plants that are not common and a few that are little cultivated are included in the hope of providing information for those who may wish to try them where conditions are suitable to their sometimes exacting needs, but also to suggest to the inexperienced the advisability of thinking twice before attempting them when there is little hope of supplying favorable growing conditions.

So far as their use in northeastern gardens is concerned, several of the plants mentioned have a limited application. Some of them, whether introduced or native, originate in regions where the winters are neither extremely severe nor prolonged, so it follows that they are better adapted to the milder southern and western states where winters are not so harsh.

Others, however, have an indispensable place in a less favorable climate. With what other equally attractive ground covers would it be possible to replace Japanese Pachysandra, English Ivy, *Vinca,* or *Euonymus,* or where find substitutes for the bright berries and pleasing foliage of American Holly at Christmas, or for Japanese Holly, or Firethorn, or some of the evergreen Barberries, to mention just a few, all with year-around good qualities? Though few may ever hope to own immense bushes of Box, such as are found in many old gardens, this plant must have a sentimental appeal for many people, or how otherwise is it possible to account for its popularity in smaller sizes?

For anyone making a garden in a region unfamiliar to him there is certain to be a period of trial and error, that is, unless he is content to use only those plants which are considered iron-hardy in the locality and to be found in most of the gardens around him. Fortunately, there is an increasing tendency to depend less on the ordinary run of plants, and many interesting subjects are available to those prepared to go to a little extra trouble, perhaps in the matter of soil preparation or winter protection, though the latter is not always necessary, except for young plants, as the geographical location or natural surroundings of the garden may provide it.

CAPRIFOLIACEAE

A B E L I A. With the exception of one or two deciduous species and the plant given below, the Abelias are not extensively grown.

Abelia grandiflora. One of the prettiest summer-flowering shrubs, but not entirely evergreen. It holds its foliage until very late in the year, usually until frost destroys it. In areas where the plant is sometimes killed to the ground in winter, shoots will come up from the base and flower throughout the following late summer and autumn, and wherever it is susceptible to cold it should be mulched in winter. Usually a shrub to 3 feet tall, though in a sheltered corner it may reach 5–6 feet. Leaves opposite, the largest little more than 1 inch long, ovate, dark green, and shiny. Flowers pale pink, ¾ inch across, produced in great numbers on lateral shoots. The small, darker colored sepals retain their color until long after the petals have fallen. The combination of small, very glossy leaves and little pink flowers in quantity is very pleasing. It is a hybrid between two Chinese species, and the hardiest of the semi-evergreen kinds.

CORNACEAE

A U C U B A. Of the very few species in this genus, *A. japonica* is the only one likely to be found in gardens.

Aucuba japonica. The normal, green-leaved form of this Japanese plant, though not rare, is less frequently seen than its var. *variegata*, Gold-dust Tree, a rather more vigorous and probably slightly hardier plant than the parent species, and in which the leaves are liberally sprinkled with yellow dots. Though not altogether uncommon, neither of them is sufficiently hardy for northeastern gardens except in a very protected position. Both require shade and will tolerate heavy shade and grow well in the smoky atmosphere of cities.

Leaves opposite, oval or elliptic, to 7 inches long and rather more than a third as wide, smooth on both surfaces and coarsely toothed, but often only on the outer half. The sexes are in separate plants, and though the flowers of neither are outstanding, those of the staminate (male) plant are pale purplish green, ⅛ inch across, in racemes 3 inches or more long, and slightly larger than those of the pistillate (female) plant. The very ornamental, ½-inch berries of the latter are in shorter racemes.

Some years ago, Aucuba was a popular conservatory and house plant when in fruit, and to ensure a good crop of berries was usually artificially pollinated. There are other varieties of *A. japonica* in addition to var. *variegata* which differ in leaf shape or manner of variegation.

BERBERIDACEAE

BERBERIS, "BARBERRY." There are a number of evergreen Barberries, the majority of them, unfortunately, tender in cold climates. Some of them also are alternate hosts of a rust disease of wheat, and these kinds may not be grown in certain states, but nurserymen know which of them are prohibited. Though some of the evergreen kinds do not differ much from one another, according to their size they are of interest in border and foundation plantings because of their generally narrow, alternate, shiny leaves with spiny margins, their conspicuous, small, yellow flowers which appear in spring in the leaf axils, and their dark-colored berries, often made more attractive by a white bloomy coating. The berries, however, because of their dark color—dark purple, blue, or black—cannot compare with the more colorful reds and scarlets of some of the deciduous species, and are further handicapped by the evergreen leaves which hide many of them.

Barberry stems are armed with exceedingly sharp-pointed, simple, or three-pronged spines, which may be a point of questionable merit depending upon how often the owner must come into physical contact with them. Where these evergreen kinds have not previously been grown the hardier ones should first be tried, as the more tender ones are liable to considerable winter defoliation and killing back of the stems, and where this kind of injury is constantly repeated the plants become dumpy and unattractive. *Berberis Julianae, B. triacanthophora, B. verruculosa,* and *B. Gagnepainii* have proved to be among the hardiest, and are sufficiently different from one another to form a good basis for trial.

Unless another country of origin is given, those that follow are from China.

Berberis buxifolia is a southern South American species, and a tall shrub with leaves 1 inch or less in length, broadest near the outer end and wedge-shaped toward the base, and merely spine-tipped, as they lack marginal spines. Flowers produced singly or occasionally in pairs, and the berries purple. The plant is apt to be badly defoliated in a severe winter, but suffers less shoot injury than some others and quickly recovers in spring. Its var. *nana* is a dwarf, rounded shrub, often under 2 feet tall, useful for foundation and similar small-scale plantings, but its value is entirely in its foliage, as flowers are rare.

Berberis candidula somewhat resembles *B. verruculosa,* but is rather hardier. Like the latter it grows slowly but has stiffer branches, and the leaves are very white on the underside. Leaves 1 inch or a little more in length, with a few spines on their margins, and the flowers usually solitary.

Berberis Gagnepainii is a spreading shrub, to 4 feet tall. Leaves narrow, to 4 inches long, with wavy, spiny margins. Flowers in small clusters, and berries blue-black with a bloom. One of the best for northern gardens.

Berberis Julianae, "WINTERGREEN BARBERRY," is upright in habit, to about 5 feet tall, with slightly angular shoots. Leaves leathery, narrow, about 3 inches long, with spiny margins, dark green above, paler beneath. Berries blue-black and bloomy. A handsome plant, it is one of the hardiest of the evergreen kinds.

Berberis Sargentiana does not greatly differ from *B. Julianae*, but is a broader plant and not quite so hardy. Shoots round in cross section. Leaves to 4 inches long, leathery, spiny margined, and paler beneath, but showing the veinlets which are hidden in *B. Julianae*. Berries blue-black and bloomy.

Berberis triacanthophora is a pretty shrub of about 3–4 feet without the stiffness of habit that characterizes some of the taller species. Leaves very narrow, strap-like, 1–2 inches long, with a few spiny teeth on their margins and a whitish bloom beneath. Berries blue-black, with some bloom. One of the best, it ranks near *B. Julianae* in hardiness.

Berberis verruculosa is an exceedingly neat, mound-like, small plant that grows rather slowly, and plants over 3 feet tall are not common in the North. It is very dense, has dark green, very shiny leaves about 1½ inches long, white beneath, and with a few spines on their margins. Small, warty growths on the shoots are a peculiarity, and its freely produced yellow flowers add to its attraction. Berries blue-black, with a bloom. Considered only as a foliage plant it would be one of the best small evergreens of any kind.

In addition to the kinds given above, the following, which are not so hardy, are more suitable for Washington, D.C., and southward.

Berberis atrocarpa, a 5-foot shrub with narrow, leathery leaves about 3 inches long, with a few spiny teeth on their edges, and black berries.

Berberis Darwinii, from Chile, is a most attractive plant 3–4 feet tall, with spreading branches, and 1½-inch leaves which are a little broader at the outer end and usually terminated by three spines, and have a few marginal teeth. The flowers are a real feature of this plant as they occur in drooping racemes to as much as 2–3 inches in length and are tinged with red. Berries deep purple.

Berberis empetrifolia is a pretty, lax little shrub of about 1½ feet, interesting for its small, ¾-inch, shiny, very narrow leaves with down-turned margins, and white beneath, and single terminal leaf spine. Flowers singly or in pairs, and black berries. It is another from South America.

Berberis pruinosa. A 6-foot shrub, with leaves to 2 inches long, shiny and dark green above, white beneath. Flowers many in each cluster, and blue-black, bloomy berries.

Berberis stenophylla. Plant-conscious visitors to England in the spring have probably noted and admired this beautiful hybrid Barberry, used as an isolated plant or in massed plantings, and to some extent for hedges. Its gracefully arching branches are enlivened in spring by the quantity of freely produced yellow flowers in small clusters. The small, 1-inch leaves are narrow, merely spine-tipped, and whitish beneath, and the berries black and bloom-covered. It may succeed further north if given a sheltered position.

BIGNONIACEAE

BIGNONIA. The plant described below is the only North American representative of this genus, though the better-known deciduous climber Trumpet-creeper, *Campsis radicans,* was, and quite frequently still is, though now incorrectly, called *Bignonia,* and a number of other plants also have borne this name.

Bignonia capreolata, "CROSS-VINE." A high-climbing plant native to some of the southeastern states which in the Northeast is liable to be defoliated, or occasionally killed back in severe winters, unless it is growing in a protected place. Leaves opposite, each composed of two leaflets 4–6 inches long, with the short stalk from which the leaflets arise extending to become branched tendrils with terminal discs. The very showy flowers, arising in the leaf axils, are in clusters of five or fewer, orange-red, funnel-shaped, and about 2 inches long.

BUXACEAE

BUXUS, "BOX." Until comparatively recently only one species of Box has been extensively grown. This one is Common or English Box, *Buxus sempervirens,* which for centuries has been a popular shrub or small tree in Europe. Much more recently the Japanese species given below and two of its varieties have become quite popular because of their greater hardiness.

Buxus microphylla is a slow-growing Japanese shrub, often rather floppy in habit, of very much smaller size—generally about 2 feet—than *B. sempervirens* and with similar, though rather narrower, opposite leaves to 1 inch long, which are rounded or notched at the apex; the shoots usually hairless. More interesting, however, is its var. *koreana,* Korean Box, which has attracted considerable attention in northeastern gardens as quite the hardiest Box. This is a small, upright plant not often more than 2 feet tall, with still narrower leaves little more than

½ inch long, which are often broadest above the middle. Its ability to tolerate winter temperatures without overhead covering, where Common Box may be injured even when provided with such cover, has made it a valuable addition in gardens where the winter behavior of Common Box may be in doubt.

Not quite so hardy is the var. *japonica,* Japanese Box, a much more vigorous shrub to 6 feet tall, but of a much looser, more open habit of growth, a trait which can be corrected by appropriate pruning. Its leaves are larger, to 1¼ inches long, and much rounder than those of var. *koreana.*

Buxus sempervirens, "COMMON BOX," "ENGLISH BOX." Stems usually minutely hairy, leaves opposite, oval, broadest below or at the middle, though the shape and size vary considerably in the varieties, about 1 inch or a little more in length, smooth and shiny on both surfaces but paler beneath, round or notched at the apex. Flowers and fruit without ornamental interest. Mediterranean region and North Africa.

Common Box is one of the most highly esteemed evergreen shrubs, so much so that its cultivation is attempted in northern areas really too cold for it even when it is provided with a protective winter covering, and south to areas where the winters do not allow a sufficient resting period. Many gardens are famous simply because of the beauty of their Box plantings, proof that qualities other than brightly colored flowers or fruits are appreciated, for Box has foliage value only. It reaches its highest degree of development in Virginia, Maryland, and the Carolinas, but has been very extensively planted further north, in increasing frequency south of New York City, on Long Island, and in Westchester County, New York, and also in Connecticut and Massachusetts, regions where the winter climate makes its successful cultivation more difficult except near the coast.

One of its valuable qualities is its shade tolerance, and in quite heavy shade it maintains its mantle of green to the ground. In warm, sunny weather it exudes a peculiar odor that is pleasant to some and equally disliked by others.

Common Box will grow in any good soil, though in a wild state it is said to occur principally in the limestone regions of southern Europe. It must not be allowed to lack water in summer; and a mulch of manure, compost, or decayed leaves, annually renewed, is very helpful.

Its most disfiguring pest is Box leaf miner, but this can be controlled by spraying with DDT or some of the newer insecticides. The timing of the spray applications is important, however, and varies with locality, so exact information on this point should be obtained from the nearest state experiment station.

Whenever there is any question of the hardiness of Common Box to a locality, it should be enclosed in winter within a framework covered with burlap or evergreen branches, and unless a permanent mulch is maintained on the soil surface, one should be provided for this season.

Common Box is naturally so dense in growth that it should not require much pruning, but it will stand close shearing and therefore is sometimes subjected to shearing where the surroundings do not justify it. When control is necessary for some of its loose-habited varieties, it is better to shorten the stronger shoots to a point just within the body of the plant than to shear them, and this kind of cutting can be repeated annually if it seems desirable.

Box was probably introduced into this country by some of the earliest settlers, many of whom brought with them representatives of the plants for which they had a particular affection. It is not surprising that in a plant so long and so widely cultivated many forms with distinctions in leaf and growth habit have arisen. Some of these varieties remain small plants, others are large and grow more rapidly than Box is given credit for in popular imagination. This belief in the slow growth of Box may be inspired by the behavior of the old, well-known variety *suffruticosa,* Edging Box, in which case it is well founded. Edging Box has smaller, oval leaves, and as its name implies is useful for edging beds and walks, in which positions it is readily kept low and neat by occasional shearing. Old plants of this variety which have been grown in positions where they could develop without crowding have considerable value.

The following are a few of the varieties of *B. sempervirens:* var. *angustifolia* is of upright and dense habit, with leaves to 1¼ inches long, but hardly ½ inch wide. Var. *bullata* has upright shoots and rounded leaves with wrinkled surfaces. Var. *Handsworthii* also has large, broad leaves, but with smooth surfaces, and is a strong-growing plant. Var. *myrtifolia* is a small bush of slow growth, with rather small leaves to ¾ inch. Var. *pendula* is tree-like in habit and very ornamental, with pendulous branches and shoots. Var. *rotundifolia* is one of the more rapidly growing kinds, usually with rather narrow outline, and is probably the hardiest of the *B. sempervirens* varieties. Var. *suffruticosa,* Edging Box, mentioned previously, is noteworthy for its very slow growth and close habit. In addition to the above there are gold and silver variegated varieties.

THEACEAE

CAMELLIA, "CAMELLIA." The beauty and value of Camellias as garden shrubs have long been recognized in southern Atlantic states, but in more northerly areas they have, until recently, been regarded as strictly cool-greenhouse plants. On Long Island, New York, and other equally favorable coastal regions, they are being successfully grown, and in increasing numbers attempts are being made further inland. One who did much to encourage their cultivation outdoors was the late Dr. P. W. Zimmerman, of Boyce Thompson Institute, Yonkers, New York, who himself experimented with them for many years. Anyone attempting to grow these plants should choose a position sheltered from prevailing winter winds, and under natural light shade.

Camellia japonica is from China and Japan. Leaves alternate, ovate, 3–4 inches long, smooth, and shiny. Flowers red, to 4 inches across, one to three in the leaf axils, though the flowers of the vast number of varieties of this plant are usually double or semi-double; some varieties are white, or various shades of pink or red, or colored flowers may be streaked with white. These varieties vary in time of flowering from early to late spring, and those which fall in the latter class are to be preferred for outdoors as the flowers are less liable to frost injury.

Camellia Sasanqua originates in the same countries as *C. japonica* and, though a rather smaller shrub, does not differ very markedly from the latter but seems to be hardier and may be distinguished from it by the hairs on the shoots and on the midrib of the upper side of the leaves. *C. Sasanqua* blooms in fall and winter, and it is reasonable to assume that those which bloom in early fall should be the more suitable for northern gardens.

COMPOSITAE

CASSINIA. Very few shrubs from "down under" are of sufficient hardiness to be of value except in the milder areas of the North American continent, and Cassinia is no exception.

Cassinia fulvida is a New Zealand shrub not of sufficient hardiness to be of importance north of Virginia. The plant has a pretty, yellowish cast due to the coating of fine hairs of this color on the shoots and the underside of the very small, about ¼-

inch, alternate, narrow, crowded leaves. The young shoots are sticky to the touch. The small flower heads are grouped many together in rather flat clusters 1–2 inches across, in the manner of many other plants of the Daisy family, but they lack the ray flowers (or petals) which make many Daisy-like flowers attractive, what color they have being due to the whitish tips of the bracts.

RUTACEAE

CHOISYA. The plant below is the only representative of the genus, but the family Rutaceae includes all the citrus fruits: orange, lemon, grapefruit, and others.

Choisya ternata, "MEXICAN ORANGE." An ornamental, rounded, Mexican shrub with opposite leaves, each composed of three wedge-shaped leaflets 2–3 inches long; and fragrant, white flowers about 1 inch in diameter, produced in axillary and terminal heads, each of four or five flowers, at the ends of the shoots. Doubtfully hardy north of Virginia except in the most favorable locations.

CISTACEAE

CISTUS, "ROCK ROSE." Small shrubs of the Mediterranean region which are very beautiful in flower. They require a very sandy, adequately drained soil—preferably on a bank or slope, as drought does not bother them—but are of doubtful value north of Washington, D.C., except, perhaps, near the coast. A sunny exposure is essential for them, and pot-grown plants should be set in permanent positions, as they are exceedingly difficult to transplant. All stimulants to growth should be avoided, as they tend to induce a soft condition more prone to winter killing. Leaves to about 2½ inches long but variable in size according to kind, in opposite pairs, those of each pair joined together around the shoot. Stems and leaves usually more or less hairy, at least on the underside. The five-petaled flowers individually are of short duration, usually about a day, but a constant succession of new flowers makes these plants noteworthy during the several weeks they are in bloom. The flowers vary in size from about 1½–3 inches in width. If only one kind is to be given a trial, *C. laurifolius* is the hardiest. Its 2½-inch flowers are white with a yellow blotch at base of the petals. Of several others the following may be mentioned:

C. albidus	flowers lilac-rose, yellow at base, 2½ inches diameter
C. hybridus	flowers white, yellow at base, 1½ inches diameter
C. crispus	flowers purplish-red, 1½ inches diameter
C. hirsutus	flowers white, yellow at base, 1½ inches diameter
C. ladaniferus	flowers white, red at base, 3 inches diameter
C. stenophyllus	flowers white, crimson at base, 2 inches diameter

RANUNCULACEAE

CLEMATIS. There are many Clematis, a few of them herbaceous perennials or somewhat shrubby, but most of them deciduous climbers in which the leafstalks, by twisting around any nearby object, serve the purpose of tendrils and support the vine. Also, the flowers are without petals, but the four, rarely more, sepals become petal-like. The fruiting heads are often almost as showy as the flowers because of the long, feathery "tails" attached to the seeds. Very few Clematis are evergreen, and the following species is the best.

Clematis Armandii. An interesting and beautiful climber from

China, but only occasionally found in northern gardens, and then suitable only for a sheltered position. The three narrowly ovate leaflets composing each leaf are 3–5 inches long, shiny, and leathery. The white flowers, to 2½ inches across, consisting of four petal-like sepals, arise from the axils of the leaves of the previous year's growth. Clematis like a slightly alkaline, rich, well-drained soil in a position providing some shade for the lower part of the stems.

EMPETRACEAE

COREMA. Of the two species of this genus only the native one given here is of interest.

Corema Conradii. A small shrub of 1 foot or a little more in height, of the coastal regions of northeastern North America, but of little importance as a garden plant. Leaves linear, heath-like, with down-turned margins, hardly ¼ inch in length, crowded on the stems. The tiny flowers occur in terminal heads, and the purple filaments and brown stamens of the male flowers are its only ornamental feature. A plant for the rock garden in very acid, peat soil, but not readily established.

ROSACEAE

COTONEASTER. Tall or dwarf shrubs which are most frequently represented in northern gardens by some of the generally hardier deciduous kinds, as few of those which are evergreen or semi-evergreen are tolerant of protracted cold weather. Though they vary in the decorative quality of their flowers, Cotoneasters are at their best when the berries ripen, those treated here having scarlet or dark red berries; in a few of the deciduous species, however, they are black. Cotoneasters can be grown in any good garden soil that is not wet, but seem to prefer one slightly on the alkaline side. They do not transplant readily so should be set in permanent positions when they are moved.

Cotoneaster Dammeri (*C. humifusa*) is a prostrate Chinese plant suitable for covering banks where there is light shade in winter; otherwise, in the North, it may be badly defoliated. The shoots run a few feet in length, and those in contact with the ground take root. Leaves elliptic, about 1 inch long, shiny on the upper surface and paler beneath. Flowers white, ½ inch across, solitary, succeeded by ¼-inch red berries, but many of the latter are hidden by the foliage.

Cotoneaster microphylla. A particularly handsome, Himalayan, small-leaved, low-growing, but eventually wide-spreading plant with stiff branches. It has more than normal attraction the year around because of its tiny, dark green leaves, about ⅓ inch long, their edges curled downward, so shiny they appear polished, but white beneath with fine hairs. The surface of the plant is abundantly furnished in spring with ⅓-inch, usually solitary, white flowers, later to become ¼-inch scarlet berries. The plant builds up slowly in height but spreads rather more rapidly, so that after many years it may be 10 feet in width. The var. *thymifolia* is generally similar in habit but smaller in its parts, grows more slowly, and has two to four flowers in a cluster.

Cotoneaster salicifolia var. *floccosa.* This variety is the hardiest of the upright-growing evergreen Cotoneasters, and may become a tall shrub. Leaves to 3 inches long, narrow-elliptic, with a wrinkled surface, and densely woolly on the underside while young. Flowers small, white, in clusters to 2 inches across, followed by ¼-inch, bright red berries. A handsome plant for a protected position in northern gardens.

Other evergreen species which are not so hardy but worthy

Cotoneaster microphylla.

of trial near the coast or further south are: *C. Franchetii, C. Harroviana, C. Henryana, C. turbinata.*

One other may be mentioned which, though not evergreen, in the North is the Cotoneaster most frequently seen in gardens, namely, the Chinese *C. horizontalis,* Fern-spray Cotoneaster. It has spreading branches on which the closely spaced branchlets form horizontal planes. Leaves roundish, pointed, ½ inch long. In spring the plant is covered with a multitude of small, pinkish white flowers, which in fall become ¼-inch, bright red berries. In a sunny position the leaves turn red in the fall before dropping. The plant may be used as a wall covering, and the red berries are very effective against a stone wall. A somewhat similar but taller plant, with stiffly drooping branches and much larger berries, is *C. apiculata.*

THYMELAECEAE

DAPHNE. With few exceptions, the hardiest of the evergreen Daphnes are what the practical gardener calls "miffy," or, to put it in everyday English, they are apt to be uncertain and difficult to grow. Most of them are best adapted to the rock garden, as perfect drainage is essential; but the soil must contain sufficient moisture in dry weather, and this is perhaps best supplied by the addition of leaf mold. Whether the majority of them prefer an acid or a sweet soil is still a rather moot point, as some growers find that one condition gives them the best results, while others recommend the opposite. For many of them a position with some protection from the sun during the hottest hours of the day is desirable. They are exceedingly fragrant. Almost all of those mentioned here originate in central or

166

southern Europe. In addition there are more tender or unreliable kinds that are not included.

Daphne Blagayana is 6–8 inches in height, with the leaves crowded at the ends of the shoots, about 1½ inches long, broadest at the outer end, tapering to the base, and shiny on both surfaces. The cream-white flowers, individually about ½ inch across, are in terminal clusters of between ten and twenty.

Daphne Cneorum, "ROSE DAPHNE." For northeastern gardens this is quite the most satisfactory evergreen kind to grow, as well as being the commonest. About 9 inches high, in time it will often form comparatively large mats of growth. It makes a mass of stems thickly clothed with ¾-inch, narrow leaves which have a slightly grayish cast. The pink flowers, about ⅓ inch wide, cluster many together on the ends of the shoots, and in season cover the plant. It is both beautiful and fragrant. In areas where it is partly defoliated in winter, a mulch of leaf mold or salt hay and a light cover of evergreen branches are probably all the protection it needs to prevent injury.

Daphne Laureola is a much taller plant, to 2 feet or more, but not so hardy, though it can be grown in a protected position. Leaves to 3 inches long, broadest toward the outer end, thick and shiny. Flowers greenish yellow, ¼ inch wide, which come in small clusters in the uppermost leaf axils. A much smaller and hardier variety is *Philippii,* with smaller leaves and flowers, the latter purplish on the outside.

Daphne pontica, from Asia Minor, usually arises from a single, basal stem to a much branched head 2–3 feet tall. Leaves shiny, to about 3 inches long, narrowing toward the base; and greenish yellow flowers, usually in pairs, at the base of the new shoots.

Daphne retusa is more tender than any of the preceding, and is a Chinese species, 1–2 feet high, with oblong leaves to 2½ inches long which are notched at the outer end. Flowers, ¾ inch across, white inside and purplish outside, grouped in many-flowered clusters at the ends of the shoots.

EUPHORBIACEAE

DAPHNIPHYLLUM. Of a number of known kinds only the one following appears to be in cultivation.

Daphniphyllum macropodum. A large shrub principally of interest for its handsome foliage, as the small, green flowers are not showy; but the plant is only occasionally attempted in the Northeast, as it is not sufficiently hardy north of Virginia. Leaves alternate, oblong, to 7 inches long, long-pointed, dark green on the upper side and whitish beneath, the leaf stalk and midrib of the leaves reddish. China, Japan.

SAXIFRAGACEAE

DECUMARIA. The plant given below has flower clusters somewhat similar to those of the related, but deciduous, *Hydrangea petiolaris* and *Schizophragma hydrangeoides*, but is without the surrounding ring of sterile flowers of the former, or the ring of single large sepals of the latter and, therefore, not quite so showy.

Decumaria barbara. A high-climbing vine for a partly shaded location in moist soil. At best it is only partly evergreen in the North, and quite often completely deciduous. Like English Ivy it clings closely to a support by aerial rootlets on the shoots. Leaves opposite, oval, 2–4 inches long; and very small, white flowers aggregated into rounded heads 2–4 inches across. A native of some of the southeastern states.

ROSACEAE

DRYAS. A small genus of suffruticose shrubs, pretty in flower and fruit.

Dryas Drummondii, "MOUNTAIN AVENS." A little plant of northern North America, forming tufts, which is hardly a shrub, as it is woody only at the base of the shoots; for alkaline soil in the rock garden. Leaves alternate, elliptic, to 2 inches long and half as wide, green and wrinkled on the upper surface, white with a felt-like coating beneath and coarsely round-toothed margins. Flowers yellow, about 1 inch wide, on stalks a few inches tall. Quite as interesting in fruit as in flower because of the numerous 1–2 inch feathery "tails" attached to the seeds. *D. octopetala* is very similar, but has white flowers. *D. Suendermannii,* a hybrid between these two, has yellow buds opening to white flowers.

ELAEAGNACEAE

ELAEAGNUS. The evergreen species of Elaeagnus are not sufficiently hardy to find common use north of Virginia, though *E. pungens* occasionally finds a place in more northerly gardens. They are interesting ornamentals covered with peculiar small scales on the leaves and young shoots. The three mentioned below are Japanese.

Elaeagnus pungens has more or less spiny, brown branches, and oblong, alternate leaves 3–4 inches long, the underside covered with dull, white scales with some brown ones among them, and undulate margins. The axillary flowers do not appear until very late in the year, October and November in Yonkers, New York, and though small—little more than ¼ inch across—and not very conspicuous, they are very fragrant, and coated with small, whitish scales. It is very doubtful whether fruits ever develop in the North. The var. *Simonii,* which differs little from the parent species except in the usually more marked silvering of the undersides of the leaves, seems to be rather hardier.

Two other species, still more tender, are *E. macrophylla,* with the young shoots and upper and undersides of the young leaves silvery scaly, the upper sides later becoming shiny green; and *E. glabra,* which becomes a climbing shrub in southern areas, is not spiny, and has brown and yellow scales on the undersides of the leaves.

EMPETRACEAE

EMPETRUM. A small genus of not very showy shrubs, principally confined to high mountains and cold northern regions, of which the following is occasionally grown in the rock garden.

Empetrum nigrum, "CROW-BERRY." A low, spreading, Heath-like shrub about 8 inches high. Leaves linear, about ¼ inch long, with down-turned edges, and crowded on the shoots. Flowers very small, purplish, in the axils of the leaves, and berry-like, black fruits hardly ¼ inch wide. It requires an acid, humus-filled, moist soil in the rock garden, but is not very adaptable to warm regions.

CELASTRACEAE

EUONYMUS or EVONYMUS. Both forms of spelling are used, but the first is now considered the correct one. Evergreen and deciduous shrubs without notable flowers, as these are rather small and either greenish or purplish in color. Most of the deciduous kinds are very showy when the colored fruits split to exhibit the seeds, each of which is enclosed in a usually orange-colored aril. Of the three evergreen species given below, the fruits of two of the varieties of one of them, *E. Fortunei*, are noteworthy, its other varieties producing fruit sparingly or not at all. In a favorable autumn *E. kiautschovica* may fruit quite well, but in northern gardens this is the exception rather than the rule. Euonymus leaves are opposite, except in one deciduous species.

Most Euonymus are very subject to attack by scale insects, and on the first signs of infestation the plants should be sprayed with malathion during the period when the young scales are moving out from under the old scales to new positions on the plant. June is the time for the first spray application in the Northeast, but correspondingly earlier further south. Unless scale insects are controlled they frequently cause defoliation, and in extreme cases may kill the plant.

Euonymus Fortunei (*E. radicans acutus*), "WINTER-CREEPER." Japan, Korea. This Euonymus and some of its varieties, which frequently are not readily distinguished from one another, are the hardiest of the evergreen kinds and those most commonly found in northeastern gardens. *E. Fortunei* is very popular as a ground cover in sun or shade, and also as a climber, clinging to its support by short aerial rootlets issuing along the shoots. Leaves elliptic, rather leathery, to 2 inches long, veins and midrib paler green, and marginal teeth. It does not fruit freely, but sometimes the small, greenish flowers are followed by green or pinkish fruits. The var. *coloratus* has found considerable use as a ground cover in recent years. Its foliage turns red in the fall of the year and provides a contrast to the usual green of plants employed for this purpose. Var. *minimus* has much smaller leaves, hardly ½ inch long, with rather strongly marked white veins, but is not sufficiently aggressive for ground-cover purposes. With still smaller leaves, of about half the size of those of *E. Fortunei minimus,* is var. *kewensis,* strictly a rock garden plant, though oddly enough if it is allowed to climb up a wall it may produce leaves more nearly the size of the parent species. Var. *gracilis* (*argenteo-marginatus*), in which the leaves are variegated with white, yellow, or pink, is also popular and sometimes used as an edging for beds and borders. It is the commonest of the few variegated forms. Much more shrubby in habit is var. *Carrierei,* which, though rather sprawling, can be grown as a quite attractive bush, and can usually be depended upon to fruit heavily. Var. *vegetus* may be grown as a bush or a strong climber and has broader, thicker leaves than *Carrierei,* but fruits equally well.

Euonymus japonicus is a Japanese species, and a rather stiffly upright, dense plant. Leaves thick, dark green, to 1½ inches long, broadest toward the outer end, with some rounded, not very obvious, teeth. It is not quite sufficiently hardy for northeastern gardens, though not uncommon, and partial shade and protection from winter winds are desirable. Without protection it is apt to be partly defoliated and suffer some killing of the shoots. It is a good plant for the coast. Its fruits are pink but not freely produced. There are a number of forms of it with variegated foliage.

Euonymus kiautschovica (*E. patens*) is Chinese, and usually only partly evergreen in the Northeast. A loosely rounded bush, 6–8 feet tall, with the leaves variable in shape but roughly broad-elliptic, to 3 inches long, with rounded teeth on their margins. Flowers small, pale green, in many-flowered open clusters from the leaf axils, and though not striking as flowers their quantity gives the bush a filmy appearance that is very pleasing. The flowers do not expand until late in the summer, a time when they are very welcome but in most northern gardens often too late to develop many, if any, fruits, which are pink, and split to expose the orange coats or arils surrounding the seeds.

ARALIACEAE

HEDERA, "IVY." Of a number of plants nowadays referred to as Ivy the name belongs more properly to the plants of this genus than to any other, and by long-established custom is applied to the English Ivy, *Hedera Helix*. Apart from differences in hardiness, the Ivies are easily grown and require a moist and reasonably fertile soil and shade.

Hedera colchica. This plant from the Caucasus and related regions is not so hardy as *H. Helix*, and should not be attempted as a climber much north of the Carolinas. It has large, very handsome ovate leaves usually without lobes, to 8 inches long. A variety of it, *dentata*, seems to be rather hardier, and commonly has a few teeth on the edges of the leaves. In Yonkers, New York, two plants of the latter in quite deep shade beneath deciduous trees at the end of several years very beautifully carpeted an area about 25 feet in diameter. The fallen leaves from the trees and the snowfalls which did not rapidly melt because of the shade from the bare tree branches supplied the necessary amount of winter protection.

Hedera Helix, "ENGLISH IVY." One of the commoner climbing plants on the north side of buildings and on tree trunks but used, perhaps, even more extensively as a ground cover in shady places, particularly under trees where grass does not succeed. As it prefers shade it is not suitable for covering build-

Hedera Helix arborescens, "TREE IVY"

ings with any southerly exposure, as such positions are too hot in summer and the foliage too prone to disfiguring injury in winter.

The leaves of English Ivy are variable in shape but roughly ovate, commonly with three to five pronounced lobes, dark green and glossy above, paler beneath, and very variable in size, to 4–5 inches long. The shoots attach themselves to a support by very short aerial roots which grow out along the shoot from that side nearest the support. Flowers are not produced until some years after the plant reaches the top of its support, at which time leaves and shoots of another kind appear. Flowers may be produced some years after the plant reaches the top of a comparatively low support, or not until it has reached the top of a tree or building. The flowers are small, green, and individually unattractive, but many of them together form an umbel, that is, the individual flower stalks are attached to a small, stalked cushion from which they radiate in all directions to form a more or less globular head which is rather unique in appearance. The succeeding berries are black. A peculiarity of the flower-bearing shoots is that the leaves are much rounder and without lobes, and usually with a more or less undulate margin. If these shoots are propagated the resulting plants do not send out long shoots, as do propagations of the typical vegetative shoots of Ivy, but grow into small bushes which begin to bear flowers when they are quite small. Plants raised from this kind of shoot are given the varietal name *arborescens*, or Tree Ivy, but it is of further interest that this type of shoot does not produce roots in the soil nearly so readily as do the vegetative shoots, for which reason it is sometimes grafted.

There are a great number of varieties of English Ivy, some of them very old and others of quite recent introduction due to a resurgence of interest in Ivy varieties during the past twenty-five years. Not all of the latter are equally hardy, and the more tender kinds are better adapted for use as house plants. Some of the newer varieties have very small leaves, branch freely, and are dwarf in habit of growth. There are a number of variegated forms. The following are some of the older, hardier varieties. Var. *baltica* is the most desirable Ivy for the northeastern region, as it is hardier than *H. Helix*. Its leaves are rather smaller than those of the latter, otherwise there appear to be no well-marked differences. Var. *Caenwoodiana* has small, very dark green leaves veined with white. Var. *conglomerata* is a low, slow-growing plant with small, three-lobed or entire leaves set closely on the shoots, and is a good rock garden plant. Var. *deltoidea* has leaves smaller than the type, triangular in general outline, but with two large lobes at the base. The leaves assume a purplish bronzy color in winter. Var. *digitata* has five, spreading, rather large pointed lobes. Var. *hibernica*, Irish Ivy, has larger, thinner leaves than the type, and the lobes tend to be shorter and broader in proportion to the size of the leaf. A handsome form, it is not so hardy as *H. Helix*. Var. *maculata* is similar to var. *hibernica*, but the leaves are variegated with pale yellow. Var. *minima* has small, closely set, three-lobed leaves, and grows slowly. The shoots will grow upright without support for a time, then they become top-heavy and fall over. It is very attractive and suitable for the rock garden. Var. *pedata* is distinct with its narrow three or five lobes, and particularly in the greater length of the middle lobe. The leaf surfaces are prettily marked with whitish veining. Var. *tortuosa* has nearly entire, curled, and twisted leaves.

Hedera nepalensis, from the Himalayas and northern India, is the most tender of the Ivies to be noted here, but can be grown in a well-protected, shady position. The leaves, to 4 inches long, take the approximate form of a narrow-based triangle with a few small lobes on each side. An attractive species, it is perhaps best adapted to the house, or, if outdoors, south of Virginia.

Hedera rhombea (*H. japonica*) has leaves to 2 inches long, usually three-lobed, the lobes broad and blunt. It is rather hardier than *H. colchica*. Japan, Korea.

CISTACEAE

HELIANTHEMUM, "SUN-ROSE." Small, low, European plants, often forming mats, which find their most fitting surroundings in a sunny position in the rock or wall garden. They require a gritty, well-drained, alkaline soil that is not enriched, as the latter practice predisposes them to winter killing. The flowers, individually fleeting but succeeded by others the following day, are attractive because of their bright colors, their numbers, and because they are held well above the low, matted foliage. There is not a great amount of difference in leaf shape between the species, and they are approximately covered by the terms narrow-oblong or elliptic. There is some confusion of names, as plants which are regarded as varieties by some botanists are treated as species by others, so a similar confusion is likely to occur in nursery catalogues. Only *H. nummularium* finds much use in gardens.

Helianthemum alpestre is low and spreading, and has leaves usually less than ¾ inch long, and often without hairs on either surface or with a few long ones, particularly on the margin; and ½-inch, yellow flowers.

Helianthemum apenninum to 1 foot high or spreading, has grayish, finely hairy leaves about 1 inch long, and white flowers of a similar width.

Helianthemum nummularium (*H. vulgare, H. Chamaecistus*). Some of the numerous varieties of this species are the Helianthemums in most common use, because they are the showiest and hardiest, but a light winter covering is advisable. Their flowers cover a range of colors: white, yellow, copper, red, some of them double. They are generally the most satisfactory because of their extreme floriferousness. In some varieties the leaves are green on both surfaces, and the undersides of others are gray with short hairs. There are also some differences in length and shape of leaf, and size of flowers, but for everyday garden purposes these are not important. The following are some of the commoner varieties:

albo-plenum	white, double
citrinum	golden yellow
cupreum	copper
diversifolium	red
"Fireball"	red
macranthum	white, yellow spot at base
mutabile	pink, sometimes streaked white
roseum	rose
rubro-plenum	red, double
stramineum	pale yellow
"The Bride"	white
venustum	crimson

CISTACEAE

HUDSONIA. One of those plants which does not take kindly to cultivation, and a constant challenge to the specialist.

Hudsonia tomentosa. A densely branched little plant of the northern seacoast and Great Lakes sand dunes, of interest only to the collector of the unusual, as it is difficult to establish or grow. Leaves very tiny, densely crowded, and overlapping on stems grayish with long hairs. Flowers about ⅛ inch in width, pale yellow, very fleeting, produced in great numbers close to the stems.

Hypericum calycinum.

HYPERICUM, "ST. JOHN'S-WORT." Shrubs with opposite, smooth leaves without teeth or indentations. The introduced evergreen, or more frequently near-evergreen, kinds are not so hardy as the deciduous American ones, and are plants for the lighter, sandy soils, as they are then less liable to winter killing. They are interesting for their summer-borne bright yellow flowers, produced singly or in clusters.

Hypericum Androsaemum, from Europe and west Asia, is 2 feet or more in height. Leaves ovate, to 3 inches long, whitish beneath. Flowers 1 inch across, usually in clusters of several flowers each. Unlike the fruits of the majority of Hypericums, which are brown, dry, and not very ornamental, this one has large, dark brown to black berries.

Hypericum calycinum grows to about 1 foot high and spreads by underground stems, for which reason it is useful as a ground cover. Leaves 2–3 inches long, whitish beneath. Flowers, usually carried singly on the ends of the stems, may be as much as 2 inches or more in diameter. The combination of low growth, large flowers, and extended period of blooming make it a most attractive ground cover, and it may be cut to the ground in early spring if it shows much evidence of winter injury. Europe, Asia Minor.

Hypericum hircinum, from the Mediterranean, is a 2–3 foot plant. Leaves to about 2½ inches long, which have an unpleasant odor when crushed. Flowers, 1 inch or a little more in width, occur singly or in twos or threes.

Hypericum Dyeri (*H. lysimachioides*) is a more tender Himalayan plant, also 2–3 feet in height. Leaves to 2 inches long, whitish beneath; and flowers 1½ inches in diameter, in clusters of several flowers each.

Hypericum Moserianum is of hybrid origin, and another attractive ground-cover plant, with arching shoots to about 1½ feet high. Leaves to 2 inches long, and flowers of about the same width in small clusters. It is not quite so hardy as *H. calycinum*, but the more ornamental of the two. A variety, *tricolor*, has the leaf edges variegated with white and pink markings, but is still less hardy.

Hypericum patulum. This Japanese species is more fittingly represented in northern gardens by its hardier Chinese variety, *Henryi*, a shrub of about 3 feet, with leaves 2½ inches long, and flowers nearly as wide. One of the showiest of the Hypericums.

Hypericum reptans is a small shrub for the rock garden, very pretty with its 1½-inch flowers produced singly on prostrate stems. Leaves ½ inch or less in length. From the Himalayas, it is not, unfortunately, very hardy and must be given winter protection in the Northeast.

There are other evergreen, introduced species of Hypericum which are not mentioned here, as they are too tender to persist for long in the northern climate.

AQUIFOLIACEAE

ILEX, "HOLLY." Evergreen or deciduous shrubs or trees with alternate leaves, and of varying degrees of hardiness, which have attracted a great amount of popular attention within recent years, to the extent that there is now a Holly society. The evergreen kinds, with their different sizes and shapes of leaf, are ornamental at all times, and those which bear red berries doubly so when the fruits are ripe. The flowers, though often numerous, are too small and lacking in color, white or yellow, to constitute much of a feature in themselves.

Hollies require a soil well supplied with acid organic matter, and as some of the tree types are not readily transplanted, liberal amounts of peat moss, decayed oak leaves, or similar material should be mixed with the backfill to aid in the rapid formation of new roots. Sometimes all the leaves are cut off American and English Hollies just previous to or immediately after planting, in order to reduce the loss of water by transpiration. This is hardly necessary if the plants are nursery-grown, have been regularly root-pruned, and are not kept out of the ground for any extended period after they are taken up in the nursery. Also, the foliage can be sprayed on both upper- and undersides with the material now so commonly used to prevent wilting. It may be advisable to prune the branches to some extent, unless the plants previously have been kept to a restricted size, but any pruning must be with due thought to the plant's eventual form. A mulch should be maintained over the root area for at least a year after planting, and a permanent mulch is distinctly beneficial. The mulch must be kept some inches away from the stems of the plants in winter, or mice may girdle the trunks.

The sexes in Hollies occur in different plants, and as only the pistillate (female) plants bear fruit, which is most important with the red-fruited kinds, it is necessary to have staminate (male) plants in addition to ensure pollination. It is stated, however, that occasionally mature plants of a given sex will carry a few flowers of the opposite sex. One staminate plant in the near vicinity of ten or a dozen pistillate ones seems to be sufficient, but this one plant need not occupy a prominent position. There does not appear to be much, if any, natural cross-pollination between species, though there are kinds in cultivation which are the result of artificial hybridization. So in order to ensure fruiting it is advisable to have plants of both sexes of each species being grown. It is impossible to know the sex of a plant until it flowers, and with plants raised from seed this takes several years. In some trials conducted at the Boyce Thompson Institute for Plant Research in Yonkers, New York, with many hundreds of seedlings of the American Holly, *Ilex opaca,* staminate plants were in the proportion of nearly two to one pistillate. For this reason and also to reduce the time required to reach fruiting age, nurserymen now raise plants vegetatively, usually from cuttings, or by grafting or budding, from plants of known sex, so that purchasers may obtain the number of each sex they require. It is also necessary to raise by these vegetative means all horticultural forms, as seedlings are unlikely to reproduce exactly the characters of the plant from which the seed is taken.

Sometimes when there are no staminate plants in the near vicinity, one or two shoots of a staminate plant are grafted onto a pistillate one in order to ensure fruit setting. With the rarer species, it is advisable to take a plant when it is available without regard to its sex.

Ilex altaclarensis. This plant is said to be a hybrid between the English Holly, *I. Aquifolium,* and a tender native of the Azores, *I. Perado.* Leaves to 4 inches long, which are longer, broader, and flatter than those of *I. Aquifolium,* therefore without the latter's attractive undulate margins, and with a very variable number of marginal spines. The shoots are dull red, very markedly so in strong, upright ones. It forms a large, dense, ornamental shrub or tree of about the same degree of hardiness as its *I. Aquifolium* parent.

Unfortunately, perhaps, it is a male plant, but there are named fruiting forms that may be of the same origin, though they are usually classified as varieties of *I. Aquifolium.* An excellent fruiting form believed to have been imported to America as a small

Ilex Aquifolium, "ENGLISH HOLLY"

plant, but probably with the same parentage, is James G. Esson, so named for its introducer, though it has also come to be known as Eldredge or Eldridge.

Ilex Aquifolium, "ENGLISH HOLLY." In its native surroundings in Britain and western and southern Europe, this plant may become a tree 40–50 feet or more in height. In those countries to which it is native, a great deal of folklore and much superstition were attached to it in the past, and it has been used there in Christmas and other celebrations as far back as recorded history.

Though generally regarded as less hardy than the American Holly, *I. opaca,* a number of quite large trees have been located in northeastern states by individuals who are intensely interested in Holly cultivation. In Oregon and northern California, where the climate is much better adapted to it, English Holly is grown in plantations, and the berry-bearing shoots are regularly harvested previous to Christmas and shipped nationwide for decorative purposes during the festive season. In England a great many varietal forms are grown, and though a number of the best of them have been introduced here, particularly in the West, they are not yet widely distributed and, no doubt, many others remain to be tried. These varieties differ in size and shape of leaf; in their greater or smaller number or absence of leaf spines; and in size and quantity, and to a lesser extent, color of berries. Many varieties have variegated foliage, with white, yellow, or blotched variegations; and there are wide differences in habit of growth, one with pendulous branches being one of the more outstanding.

The leaves of *I. Aquifolium* are oval, 2–3 inches long, dark green, shiny, and with large, hard, sharp spines on their wavy margins. The red berries are about ¼ inch in width. It is a more densely branched tree than the American Holly, and with its

Ilex cornuta, "CHINESE HOLLY"

glossier, wavy leaves is handsomer in appearance. As propagations from some of the hardiest known specimens in this country are being made, undoubtedly it will in time become very much more familiar than at present.

Ilex Aquipernyi (*I. Aquifolium* x *I. Pernyi*). Leaves about intermediate in size between the parents, though favoring *I.*

Pernyi in appearance. Will probably require winter protection in the northeast.

Ilex ciliospinosa. A Chinese species, with 1½-inch, narrowly ovate leaves with several small, spiny teeth on each margin. Berries red, almost ⅓ inch wide. Though one of the hardier kinds, winter protection is advisable until this condition is assured.

Ilex cornuta, "CHINESE HOLLY." The natural form of this species may as often be a broad, round-topped shrub as it is a tree. It is one of the handsomest Hollies, striking because of its exceedingly glossy leaves and their peculiar shape with very prominent but limited number of spines. The leaves, 2–3 inches long, are almost rectangular in outline, with the terminal leaf spine sharply turned down and the other four constituting the corners of the rectangle pointing out or up. Not infrequently another spine occurs about halfway along each side, and less often there are other variations. It fruits heavily, and the red berries are larger than those of *I. Aquifolium* or *I. opaca.* It seems probable that *I. cornuta* produces fruit without pollination, or with the pollen of *I. opaca* or *I. Aquifolium,* but does not then produce fertile seed. It has about the same degree of hardiness as *I. Aquifolium.* Yellow-fruited forms also are reported. A few varieties of *I. cornuta* are becoming available, of which the best known and no longer uncommon is var. *Burfordii,* remarkable for its very heavy fruiting and for the marked difference in leaf shape. The leaves average rather less in length than the parent, and are wedge-shaped from the broader outer end toward the base; in the number of leaf spines, usually only a terminal one or occasionally three; and in the humped-up or convex surface of the leaves. It is not quite so hardy as the parent species.

Ilex crenata, "JAPANESE HOLLY." This species and some of its varieties are the most commonly cultivated of the

Ilex crenata convexa.

hardy evergreen Hollies, and so, quite incidentally, it becomes the most popular kind with black fruit. From one variety or another a form may be chosen for any position in the garden, as its density of habit and small, neat foliage have earned it a place in the first rank of evergreen shrubs. This in spite of the fact that black berries are never so conspicuous as those of brighter color. The species is a tall shrub, 8–10 feet or taller, densely branched, but often rather narrow in outline. The leaves are variable in shape, but approximately obovate, to about 1 inch long, shiny, leathery, dark green, with indistinct rounded teeth on the margins. The berries, as already stated, are black, about ¼ inch wide, and borne in profusion. Its var. *convexa* is an exceedingly popular garden shrub, and the name is descriptive of the leaves, which are humped up or convex, and shiny. It has spreading branches, and makes a nicely rounded shrub. It is sometimes catalogued as var. *bullata.* The var. Green Island is a comparative newcomer, and is a flat-leaved, horizontally branching plant of promise. A most interesting low, close-growing, spreading plant is var. *Helleri,* which may be a yard or more wide when no more than a foot high. Its leaves, usually less than ½ inch long, are flat and much smaller than the type. Var. *latifolia* has larger, to 1 inch or more, broader leaves than *I. crenata,* but seems to be more susceptible to winter injury than most other varieties. Var. *microphylla* is one of the hardiest and most satisfactory. It has smaller leaves, ½ inch long, than *I. crenata,* and is a very neat and popular shrub. Var. Stokes is another of dwarf habit but with larger leaves than var. *Helleri,* and it appears to be less prone to winter "burning."

Ilex Fargesii. This very rare and remarkable Chinese species is distinguished by its long, narrow leaves, which may be 4–5 inches long and no more than ½–¾ inch wide, with small teeth on the outer half. It appears to be reasonably hardy, but, when available, winter protection would be advisable until its hardiness is assured.

Ilex glabra, "INKBERRY." A hardy, eastern American species, and another Holly with black berries, useful in wet or rather shady positions. It makes upright, slender, branched stems 6–8 feet tall, from underground stolons, but the clumps increase in size comparatively slowly, at least in northern gar-

Ilex glabra, "INKBERRY"

dens. Little about the plant conforms to the conventional idea of a Holly. The leaves, to almost 2 inches long, are narrow, ¾ inch or less, broadest above the middle, but narrowing to both ends, and with or without a few small teeth near the outer end; and usually of a rather light green, though the color varies. The black berries are about ¼ inch in diameter. It is another neglected native shrub which should be better known for its many uses in the garden.

Ilex latifolia is from Japan, and of very doubtful hardiness except in southern states, or possibly near the coast, but is worthy of attention where it can be grown because of its handsome, shiny leaves to 5 inches long, or even longer on vigorous young shoots (the kind of shoot most readily injured in winter!). In place of spines it has closely set small, hard, saw-like teeth on the leaf margins. The red berries are about ¼ inch wide.

Ilex opaca, "AMERICAN HOLLY." It is to this plant that most people refer when they speak of Holly. Though it is native from Massachusetts to Florida, it now seems strange that such a worth-while subject has only within the past quarter century attracted much public attention as an ornamental except by a few individuals who earlier had recognized its good qualities and decorative possibilities. Now, however, well over a hundred selections of wild or seedling forms have been given varietal names for such qualities as size, quantity, or color of berries; form and size of leaf; or the natural good habit of the plant. Not by any means are all of these many selections sufficiently hardy for northeastern gardens, and when deciding which of them to grow it is advisable to take those recommended by nurseries specializing in Hollies nearest to the area where they are to be grown. Repeated winterkilling of the shoots of kinds which are not of the necessary degree of hardiness stunts the plants and makes them considerably less attractive.

Ilex pedunculosa.

The leaves of *I. opaca* are 2–3 inches or a little more in length, oval or elliptic, dark green, but not so lustrous as are those of *I. Aquifolium,* and with large spines on the less undulate margins. The red berries are about ¼ inch wide, but half as wide again in some of the many forms. Probably of botanical rather than general interest is the fact that while *I. opaca* bears

Ilex Pernyi.

its flowers near the base of the new shoots of the season's growth, those of *I. Aquifolium* are borne on the shoots of the previous year and over a greater length of shoot. This difference is not restricted to these two species, however, as all the evergreen Hollies fall into one or other of these groups.

The American Holly is very shade tolerant though shade is

not essential, and in order to obtain the most satisfactory growth and fruiting it should be grown in positions with light, high shade, and preferably where it will receive a few hours of sunshine daily, or it may be grown in full sun.

There is a yellow-berried variety, *xanthocarpa*, which makes a striking contrast to the normal red-berried plants when they are grown together. But tradition dictates that Holly berries shall be red, so it is unlikely this yellow-fruited form will ever have the general appeal of the latter. It is also worth noting that, as with English Holly on the West Coast, there are plantations of American Holly in the East from which the berried shoots are harvested for Christmas decorations.

Ilex pedunculosa is among the hardiest evergreen Hollies, and an openly branched small tree. Leaves about 2½ inches long, ovate, dark green, and without marginal spines or teeth. After this peculiarity, its most interesting feature is the manner in which the one to three red berries in each little bunch hang from the leaf axils on slender stalks about 1½ inches long. It originates in China and Japan.

Ilex Pernyi is another Chinese species of a similar degree of hardiness as *I. cornuta*, though of much slower growth, and the leaves suggest a small form of that plant. Naturally open in manner of branching as it increases in size, the contrast between the small, closely set leaves and open habit tend to make it a plant rather unpleasantly thin in appearance, but this can be corrected to some extent by pruning. Leaves to about 1¼ inches long, leathery, shiny, dark green, with a very short leaf stalk, and usually with five spines, including the larger terminal one. The ¼-inch berries are red. Its variety *Veitchii* has rather larger leaves with more spines and grows a little more rapidly.

Ilex vomitoria is a southern native small tree commonly cultivated in Virginia and southward but not hardy further north.

Leaves to 1½ inches long, smooth, usually elliptic, with rounded marginal teeth. Berries red.

Ilex yunnanensis is Chinese and not yet common. It has ovate, pointed, finely saw-toothed leaves to 1½ inches long, and red, ¼-inch berries. At present it is rare, but when it has been propagated in sufficient quantity to be readily obtainable there is little doubt that because of its berry color it will be a valuable addition to the evergreen shrub Hollies wherever it proves to be hardy.

There are other native and introduced evergreen Hollies either too tender or too uncommon for mention here.

OLEACEAE

JASMINUM, ''JASMINE.'' The evergreen or semi-evergreen plants of this genus lack the hardiness necessary for outdoor cultivation in the Northeast, and are better adapted to Virginia and southward. None of them is as hardy as the deciduous *J. nudiflorum*, Winter Jasmine, which frequently fails to bloom in the North because the flower buds are killed, though the plant may be uninjured.

The leaves of Jasmines, in some species opposite on the shoots and in others alternate, are compound, usually with three to five leaflets, but occasionally with seven, nine, thirteen, or only one.

Jasminum Beesianum, from China, differs with one exception from other Jasmines mentioned here as it has pink flowers, whereas white or yellow is the more usual color. Unfortunately, the pink of the ½-inch flowers is not very satisfactory. The leaves have one leaflet to each leaf, are opposite, and 1–2 inches long.

Jasminum floridum, also from China, has alternate leaves, usually with three leaflets or sometimes five, each to 1½ inches long, and terminal clusters of ½-inch yellow flowers.

Jasminum fruticans, from the Mediterranean, has alternate leaves of three leaflets, occasionally only one, to ¾ inch long, and ½-inch, yellow flowers, a few together on short lateral shoots.

Jasminum humile, "ITALIAN JASMINE." Leaves alternate, of three, occasionally to seven, leaflets, to 1½ inches long; and yellow flowers of ¾-inch width, a few together terminal on the shoots. *J. humile* var. *glabrum* (*J. Wallichianum*), from Nepal, has seven to eleven, sometimes thirteen, leaflets, and more sharply angled shoots; with smaller, ½-inch, and fewer yellow flowers to a cluster than *J. humile* var. *revolutum. J. humile* var. *revolutum,* from Afghanistan and the Himalayas, is hardly evergreen, and has been known under a number of names. Its stems are slightly angular, and its alternate leaves bear five to seven or nine leaflets, each to 1½ inches long. Flowers yellow, to 1 inch across, several together terminal on the shoots and from the upper leaf axils.

Jasminum officinale, "WHITE OR COMMON JASMINE." This very fragrant and long cultivated but practically deciduous oriental species has white flowers about 1 inch in diameter in terminal clusters on the shoots. The leaves are opposite, with five to seven leaflets, each to 1½ inches long.

Jasminum Stephanense is a hybrid with pink, fragrant flowers, but is no hardier than *J. Beesianum.*

MAGNOLIACEAE

KADSURA. Of several species of this tropical Asiatic genus the following is the hardiest, and may be the only one in cultivation.

Kadsura japonica. A climbing plant from Japan and Korea, occasionally grown in the Northeast, but not of sufficient hardiness to be of much value north of Washington, D.C. Leaves alternate, to 4 inches long, narrow-oblong with a long point, smooth, and with small teeth on their margins. The ¾-inch, creamy white flowers with fleshy petals occur singly in the leaf axils, and the 1-inch berries are scarlet. It is doubtful, however, whether the showy berries are produced in northern gardens.

LAURACEAE

LAURUS. The common name of the plant given below is familiar to everyone, though the plant itself may not be.

Laurus nobilis, "SWEET BAY," "BAY-TREE," "POET'S LAUREL." Few plants have a more historic background than this one, as the Greeks and Romans are said to have formed its leafy twigs into crowns with which to decorate their most highly honored war heroes and poets. To this plant the name Laurel most rightfully belongs, though it has been used for others, notably for the American *Kalmia latifolia,* which is commonly called Laurel but more properly is Mountain Laurel, and also by a plant of Southeast Europe and parts of Asia, *Prunus Laurocerasus,* called Laurel in the British Isles, though its correct name is Cherry Laurel. Sweet Bay is a Mediterranean tree, and not reliably hardy north of the Carolinas, but it is still quite extensively grown in tubs on estates in the North for the ornamentation in summer of terraces, doorways, and similar positions, and when used for these purposes it is pruned into various formal shapes, a form of treatment of which it is very tolerant. It must be overwintered in buildings which exclude frost. Leaves oval, 3–4 inches long, dark green, rather leathery, with a pleasant odor when bruised, and, in Britain, used as a flavoring for milk puddings.

LAVANDULA. There are a number of species of this plant, most of them uncommon and too tender for outdoor planting in northern areas, but the one given below has been a favorite for centuries.

Lavandula officinalis (*L. Spica*), "LAVENDER." This old-fashioned, exceedingly fragrant little Mediterranean shrub deserves to be represented in every garden. Where there is any doubt of its hardiness it should be planted in a sunny place in rather poor, dryish soil, as it will not then grow so vigorously and be so liable to winterkilling. Usually it is not much more than a foot in height, with crowded, upright shoots and very narrow, opposite leaves, 1–2 inches long, which are covered with minute white hairs and account for the plant's grayish color. The little lavender-blue flowers appear in summer and are crowded on the upper inch or two of stalks which rise 8–12 inches above the plant. It is a very old custom to use the dried flower buds in sachets for perfuming stored clothing and linens.

LIGUSTRUM, "PRIVET." The really ornamental evergreen Privets are not hardy in the northeastern area, though some of them find extensive use further south. The decorative value of the Privets is not confined only to their foliage, as the white or cream-colored flowers of some of them are often quite showy, resembling those of Lilac but on a smaller scale. Unfortunately, they have an odor very offensive to most people. The black or purplish berries which terminate the shoots are also quite effective. All Privets have opposite leaves, without teeth. The following are among the more popular kinds sometimes given a trial in the North, but commonly grown in southern states.

Ligustrum Delavayanum, a Chinese species, is a smaller, more spreading plant than either of the following, 4–6 feet high, with shiny ovate leaves to 1 inch long, usually broadest about the middle; and little flower clusters about 2 inches long.

Ligustrum japonicum, "JAPANESE PRIVET." A shrub 7–8 feet tall, from Japan and Korea. Leaves ovate, very dark green, glossy, to 4 inches long and half as wide; short-pointed or blunt at the tip; the flower heads, to about 6 inches tall, are terminal on the shoots. Var. *rotundifolium,* often called *L. coriaceum,* is much denser and stiffer in manner of growth, with smaller, 2½-inch, rounder, thicker leaves more closely spaced on the shoots, but is no hardier than *L. japonicum.*

Ligustrum lucidum, "GLOSSY PRIVET." A taller plant than *L. japonicum,* becoming a small tree in the South. Its leaves are 4–6 inches long, somewhat narrower in proportion to their length, and more frequently drawn out to a long point than those of *L. japonicum,* with which it is much confused. Its flower clusters may be 8–9 inches long.

The two Privets commonly grown in the Northeast are California Privet, *L. ovalifolium,* a Japanese species; and Common Privet *L. vulgare,* from Europe. Neither of them, however, is entirely evergreen, and their only practical value is as hedge plants. *L. vulgare* is the hardier, but is subject to a disease which may kill not only branches, but sometimes whole sections of a hedge. *L. ovalifolium* is much the more popular of the two, as it usually retains its leaves through the winter; and it is the cheapest and commonest hedge plant—this in spite of the fact that sections of or whole hedges may be killed to the ground in severe winters.

LONICERA, "HONEYSUCKLE." The evergreen Honeysuckles are principally twining plants, and one of them is probably familiar to every gardener, as it has become an obnoxious weed in some areas.

Lonicera alseuosmoides, from China, is a climbing plant that bears some resemblance to *L. Henryi* but is not so hardy. From the latter it differs in its smooth young shoots and rather smaller leaves to about 2 inches long. Flowers yellow outside, purple within.

Lonicera Giraldii is another Chinese climber. Leaves to 3 inches long, oblong-lanceolate, with long, soft hairs on both surfaces. Shoots and flowers coated with yellow down. Flowers purplish red, to ¾ inch long.

Lonicera Henryi, also Chinese, is one of the better-known Honeysuckles, and used either as a climber or as a ground cover. Though it does not spread in the rampant manner of Hall's Honeysuckle, it requires watching to prevent it invading shrubbery or areas where its smothering growth would be harmful. Leaves oblong to lance-shaped, long-pointed, to 3 inches long, dark, dull green above, and without hairs except on both faces of the midrib and the leaf margins. Flowers purplish red, ¾ inch long.

Lonicera japonica is exceedingly fragrant and a vigorous climber. Leaves oblong, to 3 inches long, both surfaces covered with short, soft hairs when young. Flowers white, almost invariably tinged with red on the outside, 1–1½ inches long. Var. *aureo-reticulata* has the leaf veins colored yellow, and smaller leaves. It is not so hardy as its parent species, and is most frequently used as a hanging plant for window boxes, or as a pot plant. Var. *Halliana,* Hall's Honeysuckle, is distinguished from *L. japonica* by its white flowers without the red coloring, turning yellow as they age. *L. japonica* var. *Halliana* is very fragrant and beautiful with its abundantly produced flowers, but it can become a most objectionable weed. It has invaded woods and smothered the young trees, and covered and spoiled many acres of grassland.

Lonicera nitida is a neat little upright shrub, but hardly sufficiently sturdy to tolerate northeastern winters. If any attempt is made to grow it, the best location would be a well-drained position in the rock garden, though with protection it may last for several years in a border. Its principal value is for its foliage; the little ovate leaves are, as a rule, under ½ inch long. It seems to flower very little. China.

Lonicera pileata is closely related to *L. nitida,* and also from China, but is hardier and not quite so neat in appearance. It has laterally spreading branches, and leaves to 1 inch or occasionally longer. The small, whitish flowers do not add much to the appearance of the plant.

Lonicera sempervirens is the native eastern American Trumpet Honeysuckle, and usually only evergreen in protected places or mild winters. A strong climber, its leaves are variable in shape, from elliptic to oblong, to 3 inches long, with a bluish bloom on the underside. Flowers scarlet or orange, to 2 inches long, many together at the ends of the shoots.

Two other bush Honeysuckles may be mentioned, though neither of them remains evergreen in the Northeast but are of interest for their small, but very early flowers, the first of which may appear in February in mild weather. These are *L. fragrantissima* and *L. Standishii,* and they do not differ much in general appearance, though the first is a little the hardier. *L. fragrantissima* has smooth, bluish young shoots; and broad ovate leaves to 2½ inches long. *L. Standishii* has hairy shoots, and narrower, longer leaves to 3½ inches long. The flowers of both are fragrant, creamy white, and about ½ inch long.

MAGNOLIA. The deciduous Magnolias are outstanding for the spring beauty of their flowers, and the evergreen kind given below is no less noteworthy in a suitable climate.

Magnolia grandiflora, "BULL BAY." This handsome evergreen tree is a native of the southeastern United States and is commonly planted in southern gardens, where it is valued both for its foliage and its flowers. Unfortunately, it is too tender to find much use in the Northeast, unless it is trained against a wall in a protected position. The alternate leaves are 6–8 inches long, leathery, oblong or elliptic, shiny above, and covered on the underside with a rust-colored felt of fine hairs, as are the shoots. Flowers white, consisting of six, or occasionally more, thick, fleshy petals and three petal-like sepals, the flower 6 or more inches across and very fragrant.

MAHONIA. The Mahonias are closely related to the Barberries (*Berberis*), but are very different in appearance with their pinnately compound or trifoliate leaves in place of the simple leaves of the latter. Only one of them, the very decorative Oregon Holly-grape, is common in gardens.

Mahonia Aquifolium, "OREGON HOLLY-GRAPE." A most attractive evergreen shrub from Oregon and British Columbia, good in a position where it is protected from winter sun and

Mahonia Aquifolium, "OREGON HOLLY-GRAPE"

wind, and one that grows very well in light, continuous shade, such as the north side of buildings. It is a slowly spreading plant, increasing in size by sucker growth, with upright stems to 3 feet. Leaves alternate, pinnate, composed of five to nine leaflets, each of which is 1½–3 inches long, with spiny teeth on their margins. Flowers yellow, small, ¼ inch, closely clustered on 2–3 inch racemes on short, lateral shoots, which give additional beauty to the plant in spring. The fruits are blue-black berries, about ⅓ inch long, covered with a whitish bloom, and when produced in quantity are very striking. The foliage turns purplish red as winter approaches, thereby providing another interesting change. In a suitable position it is a plant hard to equal for all-round good qualities, but in winter in a sunny location it is liable to partial defoliation, at least, and the killing of the upper portion of the shoots. Where injury is less severe the leaflets may be partly killed and are then unsightly until hidden by new growth.

Mahonia Bealei is Chinese and is, perhaps, the most striking of the Mahonias. It is eventually a tall shrub, usually with a rather limited number of stiffly upright unbranched stems; with leaves, 12–15 inches long, more or less clustered at the top of the stems. The leaflets, nine to fifteen to each leaf, are also large, to 5 inches for the terminal one, and are thick and leathery, with a rather dull surface and a few spines on their margins. Flowers pale yellow, thickly set on upright stems 4–6 inches long. Berries blue-black. *M. Bealei* is sufficiently hardy, but except in the milder localities should be provided with a sheltered position from winter sun and wind.

Mahonia nervosa, from California and British Columbia, is a much lower plant, 12–15 inches high. Leaves with many—eleven to fifteen, occasionally to nineteen—spiny-edged leaflets, but it is also less hardy. Its flower-bearing stalks are twice or more the length of those of *M. Aquifolium.* Berries dark blue, bloomy.

Mahonia pinnata, another western species, is taller and tenderer than *M. Aquifolium* and better adapted to southern states. It has seven to thirteen spiny-toothed leaflets to each leaf, and the axillary flower-bearing stems are 2–3 inches long. Berries black.

Mahonia repens, also from the West, spreads by underground stems, and for this reason and because it is dwarf, 1 foot or less, and hardy, finds occasional use as a ground cover. Its leaves, however, lack the shiny surface of most of the other species and so are less attractive. The leaves consist of from three to seven bluish green, spiny margined leaflets, each 1½–2½ inches long. Its yellow flowers occur in axillary racemes, about 2½ inches long, near the ends of the stems, and it has black, bloomy berries.

One or two other more tender kinds are occasionally tried in northeastern gardens, but as a rule they do not persist for many years and are more suitable to Virginia and the South. *M. Fremontii* probably is the hardiest of these. Its leaves have three to seven stiff, spiny margined, rather small leaflets, each to 1½ inches long, which are of a very attractive blue-green color. *M. Swaseyi* has five to eleven small leaflets, each about 1 inch or less in length, and *M. trifoliata* has three blue-green, leathery leaflets to each leaf. These last two species have berries which are first red before turning black.

RUBIACEAE

MITCHELLA. This hardy and interesting little plant is the sole representative of the genus.

Mitchella repens, "PARTRIDGE-BERRY." A little trailing plant so small that only its persistent stems and evergreen leaves justify its being called a shrub. It is native to the east-

Myrica caroliniensis, "BAYBERRY"

ern states, and may be found in patches where there is shade and little other undergrowth, or in shady crevices among rocks. The stems hug the ground and root at the joints. Leaves nearly round, opposite, to ¾ inch long, usually with white lines on the surface. The ½-inch, scented, white flowers, tinged with red in the bud, are borne in pairs joined at the base, are bearded inside, and carried on short stalks which arise from the prostrate stems. The scarlet berries are about ¼ inch wide and may persist through the winter. There is also a white-berried variety, *leucocarpa.* It is a plant for the rock garden, or for use as a ground cover for small areas in shade.

206

MYRICACEAE

MYRICA, "BAYBERRY." Two Myricas are of interest for northeastern gardens, though they are not equally hardy. Their aromatic foliage alone makes them worth-while additions, and the small white or pale gray fruits are pretty in season.

Myrica caroliniensis, "BAYBERRY." This shrub is seldom entirely evergreen, but will hold its pleasantly scented foliage until winter is well advanced. There is, however, a difference in plants, as some consistently seem to lose their leaves rather early. It is a plant that has hardly received the recognition it deserves for use in mass plantings in poor, dry soils where it is often difficult to establish satisfactory growth in plants with greater eye-appeal. Its shoot growth is dense, and the leaves thickly set on the shoots, and though it is lacking in showy flowers, its hardiness and nearly evergreen qualities make it an infinitely more satisfactory plant for extremely trying conditions than subjects which merely linger because the circumstances under which they must attempt to grow are unsuited to them. It is not one of the easiest plants to move successfully, however, and if plants dug from the wild are to be used in place of those which are nursery-grown, they must be heavily cut back. There should be no difficulty in establishing plants obtained from reliable nurseries. It reaches a height of 6–8 feet, though is often smaller. Leaves alternate, to 3 inches long, usually broadest towards the outer end, and with a sprinkling of wax dots beneath. Flowers borne in small catkin-like growths, and usually overlooked. Berries, about ⅛ inch, covered with white wax. *M. caroliniensis* is native from Canada to Florida, principally in the coastal area. It was the wax obtained from this and the following species which was used by early settlers to make Bayberry candles.

Myrica cerifera, "SOUTHERN WAX-MYRTLE." An aromatic shrub or, in the more southerly portion of its range, a small tree, native to the eastern states from New Jersey southward. In the North it is evergreen only in mild winters but forms a neat bush of varying height, with alternate leaves to 3 inches long and a quarter as wide, tapering to both ends, and covered on both surfaces with minute resin glands. Flowers very small, in little catkin-like growths which are relatively inconspicuous. The tiny, white, wax-coated berries, about ⅛ inch in diameter, are a pleasing feature of this plant through late fall and winter.

BERBERIDACEAE

NANDINA. There is only one species of this plant.

Nandina domestica, "CHINESE SACRED BAMBOO." A beautiful plant in leaf and fruit that is proving to be hardier in the Northeast than anticipated, though it is much grown in the warmer southern sections of the country. It has stiff, upright stems of 3–5 feet, taller in more favorable areas; and alternate, compound leaves twice or thrice pinnate, with the leaflets varying considerably in size, the largest about 1½ inches long. Flowers white, individually small, about ¼ inch, produced in numbers in loosely arranged clusters, to 1 foot in length, which are terminal on the shoots. Berries bright red, ⅓ inch wide, which retain their good color until long after Christmas. The young expanding foliage is bronzy, and the mature foliage assumes a most attractive red color in the fall. The stiffness of its stems is offset by the delicate tracery of its foliage; and the foliage color changes in spring and fall, in addition to its long-

lasting berries, are qualitites of value in any broad-leaved evergreen. It should be given a position protected from winter
winds, and be mulched in winter in case the stems are killed to
the ground, though in eighteen years this has never happened
in the writer's experience in Yonkers, New York. A native of
China and Japan, its common name is misleading as it is not a
Bamboo, but the name is probably derived from its upright, unbranched stems.

COMPOSITAE

OLEARIA. These are shrubs of the Daisy family from
Australia and New Zealand and, as is the general rule with
plants from those regions, suitable only for areas where frost
does not persist in winter.

Olearia Haastii. A New Zealand shrub too tender for the
Northeast, though it will sometimes struggle through a few winters if given adequate protection and the weather is not too
severe; however, it is much more suitable to the Carolinas. The
young shoots and the underside of the leaves are thickly covered
with a short white felt. Leaves alternate, thick, to 1 inch long,
closely arranged on the shoots, usually rather narrow-ovate, and
blunt-pointed. Individual flowers small and Daisy-like, with yellow centers and a few white rays or petals, with many flowers
aggregated into somewhat flattened heads 2–3 inches across. A
pretty summer-flowering shrub in milder climates.

OLEACEAE

OSMANTHUS. Some species of this genus are useful
plants in the South, but only the one given here has any chance
in the Northeast.

Osmanthus ilicifolius. As occasionally seen in northeastern gardens this Japanese shrub is only a few feet in height, but in milder southern areas may exceed 10 feet. Because of its Holly-like leaves it is sometimes mistaken for that plant, but its leaves are opposite on the shoots, whereas those of Holly are alternate. Leaves oblong or ovate to 2 inches long, shiny, dark green above, paler beneath, with a few hard spines on their margins. Flowers white, quite small, about ⅛ inch, in clusters arising in the leaf axils, and fragrant. Fruits sparingly produced, dark blue, about ½ inch long, probably not produced in the Northeast. The variety *purpurascens* has purple young leaves and shoots which retain some of this color at maturity, and it is hardier than the parent species. Another variety, *myrtifolius*, is usually without marginal spines on the leaves, and there are also some varieties with variegated leaves.

ROSACEAE

OSTEOMELES. These rather uncommon plants are of use in southern gardens for their finely divided leaves as well as their small flowers and bright berries. The two Osteomeles given here are too tender to be of value in the Northeast except to those whose gardens are particularly favorably located, and even so it is advisable they be covered in winter. Their finely divided leaves are perhaps their principal feature of interest in northern gardens.

Osteomeles anthyllidifolia has thirteen to nineteen ½-inch leaflets to its alternate leaves, and is perhaps the hardier of the two.

Osteomeles Schweriniae has thinner branches, and fifteen to thirty-one grayish downy leaflets, little more than ¼ inch long, to each leaf. The nearly ½-inch white flowers occur in small, flattish clusters.

CELASTRACEAE

PACHISTIMA. Two small plants for use in the rock garden or as an edging for beds of evergreens. Ornamental for their dense growth and small foliage.

Pachistima Canbyi. A small native of the mountains of the Virginias, which should be more frequently used as a ground

Pachistima Canbyi.

cover or as an edging. The stems trail and root for a short distance, then turn upright to less than 1 foot in height, and are clothed with linear leaves 1 inch or less in length, the edges down-turned. Flowers, small and reddish, from the leaf axils, but hardly to be described as showy.

Pachistima Myrsinites is from the West and may grow twice as tall as *P. Canbyi;* its leaves are broader and its small flowers greenish, but it is not quite so hardy as the foregoing.

BUXACEAE

PACHYSANDRA. Of the two species given below, the Japanese is much the better known and to be preferred for the purpose to which they are usually applied, that of ground covers.

Pachysandra procumbens, an American species, is not usually evergreen, at least in the North, where late in the winter the shoots fall over and with the leaves eventually decay, nor is it quite such an attractive plant as the Japanese. The leaves are dull green, broader, and with still larger teeth, but otherwise it is very similar in appearance to *P. terminalis.* It does, however, produce flowers more regularly in early spring. Upright spikes, to about 4 inches tall, arise from the base of the old shoots and bear many small, pink flowers, which are quite showy.

Pachysandra terminalis, "JAPANESE SPURGE," "PACHYSANDRA." This is one of the most useful and popular ground covers for shade in northeastern gardens. The shoots rise to a height of 9–10 inches from underground stems and are leafy only near the top of each year's growth. The alternate leaves are broadest and coarsely toothed at the outer end, 3–4 inches long, smooth, and shiny. In some years the white, small flowers are quite freely produced, and though the spikes are

Pachysandra procumbens.

terminal on the shoots they cannot be said to add much to the appearance of a planting. The berries, which are comparatively uncommon, are little more than ¼ inch in length, and are whitish and translucent. In half shade or quite deep shade this plant has an excellent dark green color, and becomes dense enough to crowd out all but an occasional weed. When growing in the sun, the leaves are smaller and their yellowish color not at all pleasing. Though it spreads by underground stolons it is quite readily kept within bounds. It is native to Japan. There is also a variegated form of it.

ROSACEAE

PETROPHYTUM. The little plant given here appears to be quite uncommon, and is adapted only to a crevice in the rock garden.

Petrophytum caespitosum (*Spiraea caespitosa*). A very neat, grayish little plant of mat-like growth, of not more than 1–2 inches in height. The leaves are narrow, broadest toward the outer end, not much more than ½ inch long, and coated with soft, fine hairs. The tiny, yellowish-white flowers are crowded at the top of stems 2–3 inches tall. From the middle northern states.

OLEACEAE

PHILLYREA. The Phillyreas are not sufficiently hardy for the Northeast, and only in more favored southern locations do they offer competition with many superior broad-leaved evergreens. All have opposite leaves, and the flowers are axillary on the shoots of the previous year. They originate in the Mediterranean region and West Asia.

Phillyrea angustifolia. A shrub with linear leaves, 2–2½ inches long and about ⅜ inch wide, smooth on both surfaces but paler beneath, sometimes with a few small marginal teeth. Flowers small, greenish white. Fruit small, black, berry-like.

Phillyrea decora. This is commonly said to be the hardiest species but seems to be no more reliably hardy than the others. Its leaves are leathery, oblong, 3–4 inches long, tapering to both ends, shiny and smooth on both surfaces. Flowers white, ¼ inch wide, many in the clusters.

Phillyrea latifolia. A large, rounded shrub where the climate permits of its free growth. Leaves 1½–2½ inches long, ovate, short-pointed, smooth, dark green, paler beneath. Flowers whitish in small clusters. Fruit ¼ inch wide, blue-black.

ROSACEAE

PHOTINIA. Of several Photinias, deciduous or ever-green, the one given here is a handsome plant for southern gardens.

Photinia serrulata. A handsome Chinese shrub, or a small tree in southern climates. It is too tender to be of value in the North-east except, perhaps, near the coast. It has dark green, alternate, oblong, shiny leaves, as much as 7–8 inches long, finely saw-toothed on the margins. The red, expanding young foliage is particularly striking in contrast to the older green. The flowers are white, ¼ inch wide, in large clusters, which are succeeded by ¼-inch red berries.

POLYGALACEAE

POLYGALA. The following is one of the woody stemmed exceptions among a great number of species which are usually herbaceous perennials, and include many North American kinds.

Polygala Chamaebuxus. A small, creeping shrub, but not one of the very hardiest, of less than a foot in height, with pretty Pea-like flowers. Leaves alternate, elliptic, to 1 inch long, dull green, and rather leathery. Flowers cream-colored, sometimes with a reddish keel, and about ½ inch long. The superior variety *grandiflora* has flowers with purple wings and a yellow keel. A plant for rather sandy or calcareous soils, with some shade during the hottest hours of the day. From Switzerland and Austria.

ROSACEAE

PRUNUS. With the exception of a very few of the varieties of *Prunus Laurocerasus,* the evergreen kinds of this genus are too tender to be of use in the Northeast.

Prunus Laurocerasus (*Laurocerasus officinalis*), "CHERRY LAUREL." This plant of Southeast Europe and Asia Minor is not sufficiently hardy to be of use in northeastern states, though extensively grown in the Pacific Northwest, and also south of Virginia, where it may make a plant 12–15 feet tall and as much in width. It is quite shade tolerant and will stand hard pruning, a form of treatment to which it is often subjected in Britain, where it is much used in massed plantings that are kept to a height of 3 or 4 feet, but such hard usage is increasingly condemned. It has handsome, dark green, shiny, alternate, oblong or partly obovate leaves with some indistinct marginal teeth, to 6 inches long. The ⅓-inch, yellowish white flowers are produced on upright spikes to 5 inches long, and are followed by ½-inch dark purple berries. A few of its varieties are much hardier than the species, and are not at all uncommon in north-eastern gardens where the winters are too severe for the parent plant. Var. *schipkaensis,* a much smaller plant with smaller leaves, to 4½ inches long, and smaller flower spikes, seems to be quite the hardiest variety. Var. *serbica* is of more upright growth, the leaves usually broadest toward the outer end and with a wrinkled surface. Var. *Zabeliana* is distinguished by its very narrow leaves and upright, rather stiff manner of branching.

Prunus lusitanica, "PORTUGAL LAUREL." In general appearance this plant does not markedly differ from *P. Lauro-cerasus,* but it is less hardy and there appear to be no forms of it which are hardier than the species, so that only south of Virginia and on the northwest coast is it of importance. From the previous plant it is distinguished most readily by its very much longer flower spikes, which are about twice as long as in *P. Laurocerasus.*

Prunus caroliniana, native to some southern states, is too tender to be of much value north of North Carolina, though it is occasionally tried in the Northeast.

ROSACEAE

PYRACANTHA, "FIRETHORN." The Pyracan-thas are particularly handsome in fruit, but, unfortunately, only one of them, the Laland Firethorn, can be considered hardy in the Northeast. Others are better adapted to more southerly areas. They resent transplanting, for which reason they are often set out from pots, though they may be moved successfully if they have been frequently transplanted in the nursery, and require a soil adequately drained. They have alternate leaves and usually spiny branches.

Pyracantha coccinea is a 6- to 8-foot, exceedingly thorny shrub, handsome when in fruit. Leaves oval to oblanceolate, to 1½ inches long, usually with finely saw-toothed margins. The white, ⅓-inch flowers occur many together in flattish heads which become clusters of bright red, ¼-inch berries in the fall. Laland Firethorn, *P. coccinea Lalandii,* is a hardier, taller, more loosely branched plant, very striking in appearance when bearing its still more abundantly produced but orange-red berries. Both are excellent wall plants, but except when planted in a frost pocket *Lalandii* is usually quite satisfactory in an open border. South Europe and Asia Minor.

Other Pyracanthas more suitable for Maryland and the South are: *P. atalantioides* and *P. crenulata,* though two of the varieties of the latter, namely *kansuensis* and *Rogersiana,* are hardier than the parent species and may be grown in New Jersey and Long Island, New York.

L A B I A T A E

ROSMARINUS. This Mediterranean shrub, the only one in the genus, is not so hardy as Lavender, but like it has been cultivated in Europe for an indefinite period and is an old, old favorite among aromatic plants.

Rosmarinus officinalis, "ROSEMARY." Too tender for the Northeast, except perhaps near the coast or some other equally favorable location, though it will sometimes live for a number of years if it can become established in a well-drained, rather poor soil in a sunny but sheltered position. About 18 inches tall, though it will grow to two or three times this height in more southerly states, it has upright, downy branches, opposite, very narrow leaves to 1 inch long, with the edges turned down, coated on the underside with fine, white down. The blue flowers come in the axils of the leaves on the upper ends of the previous year's shoots, and are about 1 inch long.

LILIACEAE

RUSCUS. Of the few species in this genus only Butcher's-broom is at all common. It is said to have derived this common name from its old-time use by English butchers, who tied several stems together and used them as a broom with which to clean their chopping blocks or floors.

Ruscus aculeatus, "BUTCHER'S-BROOM." A curious plant of 1–2 feet in height, curious because the members which appear to be leaves are actually flattened branches, or cladodes, leaf-like in shape and serving the function of leaves. The true leaves are very small and bract-like, and only to be detected on rather close inspection. The stiffly upright, grooved stems arise from an underground root-stock; the cladodes are thick, ovate, about 1 inch long, with a hard, spiny tip. The flowers are very small and appear in the middle of the cladodes; the sexes are in different plants, and unless plants of both are growing together, the red, ½-inch berries are not produced. Best adapted to the Carolinas and California. In the North, it may occasionally be found in deep shade in a protected place in some gardens. In the milder sections of the country it is extensively grown for Christmas decorations and may be marketed in the natural green state or, more frequently, dyed red. As it does not drop its cladodes when they are dry it remains useful for a long time. Native of southern Europe.

RUTA. The following is the only commonly cultivated species of several, which are principally from the Mediterranean region.

Ruta graveolens, "COMMON RUE." A plant of unpleasant odor and very unpleasant taste but an ancient medicinal plant, therefore, perhaps, belonging more properly to the herb garden than the border. However, its alternate, doubly pinnate, finely divided, smooth leaves have an attractive bluish green shade that justifies its inclusion in a herbaceous border. If much handled, it is very irritating to some tender-skinned persons. One–2 feet in height, rather more when the terminal flower heads appear. Flowers yellow, about ¾ inch wide. Europe.

COMPOSITAE

SANTOLINA. The plants given here are the commonest of a few species, and the first has long been a favorite for low edgings and formal summer bedding because of its attractive light gray foliage and small size.

Santolina Chamaecyparissus, "LAVENDER COTTON." Better suited in the Northeast to its common use as a summer bedding plant, when it can be overwintered in cold frames, than as a garden shrub, though in a poor, rather dry soil it may live for many years. A dense little plant of 1 foot or a little more in height, its almost white, odorous foliage its feature of interest. The alternate, finely hairy, pinnate leaves to 1½ inches long have very many, very narrow tiny leaflets. The yellow flowers,

Sarcococca Hookeriana humilis.

without rays or petals, have little ornamental value so are usually cut off. A somewhat similar plant, but with green, hairless leaves and not so hardy, is *S. virens*. Both are from southern Europe.

SARCOCOCCA. Though related to Box these plants are quite different in appearance, but with pleasantly scented though rather inconspicuous flowers.

Sarcococca Hookeriana var. *humilis* is a small Chinese shrub and, while not common, is used to some extent as a ground cover, or in clumps, in shady positions. Of rather low stature, 18–24 inches, it has upright stems from an underground rootstock which does not rampantly spread. Leaves alternate, narrowly ovate, pointed, shiny, rather leathery, 1½ inches or rather more in length. Flowers quite small, whitish, a few together in small clusters, male and female flowers separate but in the same cluster, and the subsequent black berries about ¼ inch in diameter. Its neat, glossy foliage and shade preference are qualities which have not yet been widely appreciated. It may not be sufficiently hardy in areas where winter temperatures frequently go below zero.

Sarcococca ruscifolia is not so hardy as the plant given above, and not common, but rather taller, with larger ovate leaves to 2½ inches long and dark red berries.

RUTACEAE

SKIMMIA. Skimmias do not find much use in the Northeast, as they are not quite sufficiently hardy, but probably they could be employed more frequently in shade on ground with sufficient slope to provide good air drainage.

Skimmia japonica. A Japanese shrub very beautiful when in

fruit, but as the leaves turn an unpleasant yellow when exposed to the sun, shade is necessary during the sunniest hours. Usually not more than 2–3 feet tall, it makes a rounded shrub, with alternate leaves speckled with almost transparent dots. Leaves to 4 inches long, oblong, or sometimes broadest toward the outer end; and terminal-flower clusters to 2–3 inches long, composed of many small, pale yellowish, fragrant flowers. The sexes occur on different plants, and the staminate flowers are the more heavily scented, which originally gave rise to the belief that it was a distinct species; and it was named S. *fragrans*. In order to obtain fruit, plants of both sexes must be present. The ½-inch berries are bright red.

Skimmia Reevesiana, a Chinese plant, is smaller and rather hardier than S. *japonica* and usually has perfect flowers; therefore any one plant may be expected to fruit, and for this reason alone it is to be preferred, though better pollination is to be expected when two or more plants are grown together. But the oval berries do not have quite the same bright color as those of S. *japonica.* Formerly both species were common cool-greenhouse plants, and in order to insure good crops of berries artificial pollination was often resorted to. A hybrid between these two is S. *Foremanii.*

R O S A C E A E

S T R A N V A E S I A . Of a few species the following appears to be the only one in cultivation.

Stranvaesia Davidiana. A very loosely branched, rather straggling shrub 6 feet in height, probably more in the milder sections. Leaves alternate, to 4 inches long, approximately lance-shaped, or broadest toward the outer end. Flowers in flat, loose heads to

3–4 inches in diameter, the individual flowers white, ⅓ inch across, followed by pink berries about the same size. The variety *undulata* is hardier, and a smaller, more spreading plant with smaller leaves having undulate margins. The underside of the leaves of S. *Davidiana,* and more particularly those of var. *undulata,* turn dark red in the fall of the year. This feature and the color of the berries, which are pink rather than red, are the best features of an otherwise not very ornamental subject. Both are Chinese, and prone to some injury in severe winters.

HAMAMELIDACEAE

SYCOPSIS. The species given here is little known, but because of its shiny evergreen foliage may eventually prove to be a good garden shrub wherever it is hardy.

Sycopsis sinensis. An uncommon Chinese shrub, the principal merit of which seems to be in its foliage. The alternate leaves, 4 inches or less in length, are rather narrow and drawn out to a long point, have a few very small teeth on the margins, and are smooth on both surfaces. The small flowers are said to be unimposing except for their red anthers, but appear very early in spring. In the Northeast requiring winter protection until its hardiness is assured.

LABIATAE

THYMUS. There are a number of Thymes, but also some confusion of names, as some that are regarded as species by one botanist are varieties to another. The two given here are the most common.

224

Thymus Serpyllum, "MOTHER-OF-THYME." A little, tufted, half-shrubby plant familiar to everyone, sometimes used as an edging, or as a ground cover for sunny banks, but more frequently between crevices in stone steps and flagstone walks. Its prostrate stems root as they run. Popular because of its fragrance when bruised or crushed, or when the air is still and warm. Leaves opposite, oblong, hairy, usually under ½ inch long; and small purple flowers crowded into heads terminal on the shoots. There are a number of varieties, and for color of flowers one of the best is *coccineus,* in which they are scarlet. Var. *albus* has white flowers, and the foliage of var. *lanuginosus* is gray with woolly hairs. Var. *aureus* has variegated foliage, and var. *vulgaris* (*T. citriodorus*) is the Lemon Thyme.

Thymus vulgaris, "COMMON THYME." This is a pot herb to be found in all herb gardens and known to every housewife, if only in the form of the dried, crushed leaves used for seasoning, but because of its aromatic fragrance sometimes planted in the border. Unlike *T. Serpyllum,* it is upright in habit to 6 inches or a little more, and its ½-inch leaves are whitish beneath with fine hairs. Both species are southern European.

TROCHODENDRACEAE

TROCHODENDRON. There is only one species in this genus.

Trochodendron aralioides. A rather striking evergreen shrub, eventually a tree, from Japan and Korea, that is proving to be hardier than anticipated, but even so it should be given a sheltered position until its hardiness is proved. It has leathery, alternate leaves, the largest 6 inches long, dark green on the upper surface, much paler beneath, toothed on the margins, and long leafstalks about half the length of the blade. The large, pointed, terminal winter buds are usually red. Flowers green, ¾ inch wide, but without petals, the stamens and pistils forming the showy part of the flower; in terminal racemes 2–3 inches high.

CAPRIFOLIACEAE

VIBURNUM. A large and ornamental genus from the garden standpoint, though most of the species are deciduous, and almost all of those which are evergreen best adapted to Virginia and southward.

Viburnum macrocephalum var. *sterile,* "CHINESE SNOW-BALL." A tall shrub which provides the largest snowballs of the three Viburnums peculiar for this kind of flower head. It is the globose heads, rather than flat, of entirely sterile flowers, which are many times larger than the more normal flowers which bear sexual organs, that makes them noteworthy. In the Chinese Snowball the globose heads may be almost 6 inches in diameter, with the individual flowers about 1 inch across. As the plant is tender, it requires adequate protection in the Northeast, which is perhaps best provided by training it against a sheltered wall. It is usually only partly evergreen, or in cold winters entirely deciduous.

Viburnum rhytidophyllum. This is the hardiest of the evergreen Viburnums, and quite popular. An upright Chinese shrub of 6–8 feet, the young stems heavily felted; leaves opposite, oblong, to 7 inches long, glossy, but very wrinkled on the upper surface, and with a yellowish felt-like coating beneath. Flowers yellowish, individually about ¼ inch across, produced in flattened heads 4 inches or more in diameter. As is common to many of the Viburnums, the fruits turn from green to red, then to black. For the sake of its foliage it should be planted where it receives protection from winter winds, and light shade is also desirable. In the summer it is a handsome plant, and if any objection can be raised to it, it is to its look of dejection in the depth of winter, as the leaves hang down as though without hope of another spring! There are other evergreen Viburnums suitable for the milder winters of southern states, among which may be mentioned, *V. Davidii, V. Henryi, V. japonicum, V. odoratissimum, V. Tinus,* and *V. utile.*

APOCYNACEAE

V I N C A . Each of the two small shrubs given here is of considerable usefulness in the area to which it is adapted.

Vinca major. This trailing plant in not hardy outdoors north of Virginia, but in northern states is much used in either the normal green or the variegated form, var. *variegata,* in hanging baskets or window boxes wherever there are cool greenhouses or cold frames in which it may be overwintered. Leaves opposite, oval, shiny, to 2½ inches long, and pretty blue flowers, to 1¼ inches across, which arise from the leaf axils.

Vinca minor, "PERIWINKLE," "MYRTLE." Along with Japanese Pachysandra and English Ivy this plant must be rated as one of the hardiest ground covers for shade in northern gardens, and has an advantage neither of the others possesses, that is, really showy flowers over a long season, though the greatest display is in spring. So well has it adapted itself to this climate that, though originally from Europe, it is not uncommon to find it growing wild in shady places. Leaves oblong to ovate, to 1¼ inches long, dark green, and shiny. Flowers bright blue, about 1 inch across. *V. minor* has given rise to a number of varieties, some of which are: *alba,* with white flowers; *atropurpurea,* purple; and *multiplex,* double purple. In addition there are forms with variegated leaves.

LILIACEAE

YUCCA. The Yuccas are essentially plants of the semi-arid regions such as the southwestern states and Mexico. A few, however, are native to or extend to sections of the Southeast, and among these are some that may be grown in a more northerly climate. Because of their affinity for the drier, sandy soils, in northern areas, sites which are adequately drained must be chosen for them. Soils which hold a great amount of water during the winter months are unsuitable because of the possibility of frost injury to the plants and their subsequent decay. In the manner in which their many long, narrow leaves are produced from the top of a stem which in the hardier kinds hardly rises above the ground, and in their immense, upright flower-bearing stalks, Yuccas are quite distinctive among woody plants. The individual flowers are pendulous, greenish white, or creamy white, and quite large, some to about 3 inches long, and a great many to each inflorescence.

Yucca filamentosa, "ADAM'S NEEDLE," "SPANISH BAYONET." This is the Yucca most frequently found in northern gardens, and the most reliable in production of flowers. It has no very obvious stem. The stiff leaves are 2–2½ feet long, 1½–4 inches broad, glaucous-green, with loosely twisted fibrous threads along their edges. The flower stalks are 4–8 feet or occasionally more in height, with the flowers in panicles, that is, on short branches arising from the main flower stalk.

Yucca flaccida. A rather smaller plant than the last, with more flexible leaves with a bend in them, 1½–2 feet long, to 1½ inches broad, gradually drawn out to a point, and with straighter marginal threads. The panicles rise 3–4 feet but are not usually so wide as those of *Y. filamentosa.*

Yucca glauca. One of the hardy species that may develop an above-ground, definite stem, but it rests on the ground. The leaves are 2 feet or a little more in length, very narrow, about ½ inch, with a narrow white edging and a bloomy coating, and some fine marginal threads. Inflorescence narrow, usually without branches, raceme-like, to 3 feet tall.

Yucca gloriosa is one of the most attractive, and may sometimes form a short above-ground stem. Leaves to 2 feet long, 2 inches or a little more in width, usually without or, as they age, with a few threads on their edges, with a bloomy coating, and ending in a sharp spine. Flower stems 3–4 feet tall, with short flowering side branches, flowers large, sometimes tinged with red. Best adapted to North Carolina and southward.

Yucca recurvifolia. In the warmer areas this species forms an upright and eventually branched stem. Leaves to 3 feet long, to 2 inches broad, with a bend in them, and glaucous. Flower stems to 3 feet tall, forming a narrow panicle. Not reliably hardy north of the Carolinas.

8 The Heath Family or Ericaceae

The plants of the Heath family are merely a part of the broad-leaved group, and the more logical treatment of them would be to distribute the various genera alphabetically throughout that group. The excuse for devoting a chapter to them is sought in their general requirement of an acid soil containing an ample supply of organic material, as was pointed out in Chapter 3. Allotting them a separate chapter may help to impress these needs on the mind of the reader. For most of them, the most suitable soil is that within the range pH 4.5 to pH 5.5, which is well below the neutral point, pH 7.0. For a few kinds not commonly cultivated, it must often be close to the lower figure.

For the majority of the shrubs of this family, the addition to a naturally acid soil of sufficient organic material of a kind that will maintain the acidity should ensure success. But if there is any doubt about the necessary degree of the soil's acidity it is advisable to have it tested, as the line between successful and indifferent culture is often a matter of small but usually important details.

Soil-testing kits are available at moderate prices with which the homeowner is able to determine for himself the degree of acidity or alkalinity of his soil. They are simple to operate, but in order to obtain reliable and comparable readings the instructions which accompany them must be strictly followed. County agricultural agents and state experiment stations will also supply the information if a soil sample is sent to them. These agencies usually provide a form to be filled out, with instructions as to how the soil samples are to be taken. For a fee the tests are also made by private agencies.

Too often such plants as Rhododendron, Mountain Laurel, Pieris, and others are to be seen with yellow, undersized leaves, leggy stems, and a minimum of annual growth, usually in conjunction with an almost total lack of flowers. Several causes may be responsible, but in the East, except in limestone regions, the soil is usually on the acid side, and a much greater probability of poor plant behavior is due to an inadequate amount of organic matter in the soil. Peat moss, decayed Oak leaves, decayed Pine needles, or decayed hardwood sawdust, all of which prevent the soil from packing and thereby permit the necessary amount of air to enter, also encourage the multiplication of roots in plants of this group, so should be added in liberal quantities, particularly in close-textured and rather heavy soils.

Another reason for unsatisfactory growth may be inadequate soil drainage, which is likely to occur in a clay soil, over a clay subsoil, or in low ground, where too many of the fine, hair-like roots will decay during those periods when the ground is more or less waterlogged. Contrarily, poor growth of these plants in foundation plantings or in very light soils may be due to an insufficient supply of moisture at the roots. Even though the eaves of a house do not overhang more than the average of a few inches, the ground near the walls may be much drier than the householder ever suspects. But when they overhang two or three feet, as in some modern dwellings, an almost desert-like condition may occur. Here again the spongy, water-holding ability of organic materials, both in the soil and as surface mulches, is invaluable but must be supplemented by adequate supplies of water, especially during the time of active growth in spring and early summer, and again before winter sets in.

Public water supplies are often alkaline, as are some well waters, and where it is necessary to use these sources of water in quantity to maintain the soil moisture, in time they will begin to show their deleterious effect on the plants. As the soil becomes gradually more alkaline the plants show progressive signs of deterioration, and until the cause is realized these signs are often hard to account for, particularly when every care may have been taken with the initial preparation of the affected areas and growth has been satisfactory for some time after planting.

Sufficient lime may be gradually washed from the walls of stucco houses, and to a lesser extent from those of stone or brick, to reduce the acidity of the soil around house foundations, and for any of the above reasons an occasional check on its pH is advisable.

Not all of the plants mentioned in this chapter are subjects for every garden. A number of them are difficult to establish and grow, consequently there is little demand for them and they are not always readily obtainable; but even though the reverse were true, some of them would not meet the decorative needs of the average garden—rather they are plants for the specialist or the collector of the unusual. Others, however, are familiar to everyone and exceedingly pleasing whether in or out of bloom, and justify any extra effort required to bring out their true decorative qualities.

ANDROMEDA. This name is now confined botanically to the two plants given here, though it is used as the common name for two others quite common in gardens, namely Japanese Andromeda and Mountain Andromeda, but their correct botanical name, *Pieris*, should be substituted for *Andromeda*.

Andromeda Polifolia, "BOG ROSEMARY." A small bog shrub of northern North America, and of similar climates in Europe and Asia, principally of interest in a collection of Heath plants or a wet spot in the wild garden. It has wiry stems, 1 foot or more in height, from a creeping rootstock. Leaves opposite, very narrow, 1–1½ inches long, with down-turned margins, and with a white bloom on the underside. Flowers individually small, ¼ inch long, urn-shaped, pink or white, in clusters of a few flowers at the ends of the shoots. The similar *A. glaucophylla* is not quite so attractive, and is less often seen in gardens. It has a covering of very short, fine hairs on the underside of the leaves.

ARCTOSTAPHYLOS. There are many shrubs of this genus, but the others, of the few in cultivation, are suitable only for California and similar climates.

Arctostaphylos Uva-ursi, "BEARBERRY." A completely prostrate plant of North America, common on the northeastern coast, and of Europe and northern Asia. It grows in the poorest kind of sandy acid soil, often where little else will grow, and forms a beautiful ground cover for sandy banks. Leaves about 1 inch long, opposite, shiny, obovate, and blunt-ended. Flowers pinkish, urn-shaped, barely ¼ inch in length, occurring in short racemes of a few flowers each, and followed by small, shiny, red berries. Unfortunately, it is not readily transplanted except from pots, and even when this precaution is taken it is not always easily established. Where it can be obtained from the wild it is sometimes taken up as frozen sods, or as thick turfs in spring, and set in planting sites prepared by mixing peat moss or other acid organic material and sand with the soil. Frozen sods are prepared by digging narrow trenches between the sods late in the fall of the year before the ground freezes. After the sods are frozen through, they can be taken up without disturbing the roots. When conditions suit it, it seems to be insect- and disease-free, forms a dense carpet on the ground, and will grow in full sun or partial shade.

BRUCKENTHALIA. The small shrub given here is the sole representative of this genus, though in the past it was included with *Erica*.

Bruckenthalia spiculifolia, "SPIKE-HEATH." A dwarf, dense little plant about 6 inches high, with upright shoots which in due season are terminated by very short racemes bearing ⅛-inch, light pink, bell-shaped flowers crowded together. Leaves very narrow, heath-like, about ⅙ inch long, thickly arranged on the stems. Like its near relatives the *Ericas* and *Calluna* it is more effective when planted in groups than singly. Native to Southeast Europe and Asia Minor, it should be given a position adequately drained in winter, and in most northern areas the protection of a covering of salt hay or evergreen branches.

CALLUNA. The shrub given below is the only one in the genus.

Calluna vulgaris (*Erica vulgaris*), "HEATHER," "LING." A low shrub of Europe and Great Britain where it covers thousands of acres of acid moorland which become seas of purplish pink when the plants bloom in August and September. It is an old but still popular belief that to find a sprig of white Heather growing among the acres of purple is extremely lucky. Normally a plant 1–1½ feet in height, sometimes taller, the branches densely clothed with very tiny, about 1/10 inch long, scale-like leaves. In spring the shoots lengthen and branch to become flower-bearing stems on which the tiny flowers are thickly clustered. In some of the numerous varieties of this plant the flower-bearing portion may be 8–12 inches long, but in the wild form is usually about half that length. The flower color is commonly described as purple, "the bonnie purple Heather," but in the varieties, many of which are much more ornamental than the parent, ranges from white through pink and red to crimson, for which reason they are more commonly planted than the species. In spite of the fact that *Calluna* has become naturalized to a very limited extent in parts of eastern North America and is not uncommon in gardens, it is apt to suffer injury in severe winters until such time as it is well established and completely covers the ground, and before this occurs a winter covering is advisable. Planting on a slope is preferable to flat ground, for though moisture in the soil is essential, in winter in the northern climate water should never stand about their roots. The plants should be sheared in spring before growth commences, in order to keep them low and induce greater density of branching, a practice which also seems to increase their ability to withstand winter cold. Among the more ornamental varieties are:

alba minor	white, medium height
alba pilosa	white, tall, grayish coating of short hairs
Alportii	crimson, tall, one of the best
atrorubens	crimson, medium height
coccinea	crimson, tall
cuprea	purple, medium height, golden foliage in summer, bronze in winter
Foxii	pink, very dwarf, does not always flower freely
Hammondii	white, tall
plena (*multiplex*)	pink, double, like minute double-flowered roses
Searlei	white, tall, one of the latest and showiest

CASSIOPE. Cassiopes are rock garden plants for the specialist, and require a cool position, moist, peaty soil, and shade, at least during the hottest hours of the day. The arctic kinds suffer from summers that are overlong for their best welfare.

Cassiope hypnoides is a small plant, 2–3 inches high, often with procumbent stems, of arctic or cool, high mountain regions of northern North America; with very small, rather scale-like leaves, and ¼-inch white or pinkish nodding flowers borne singly at the ends of the shoots. *C. Mertensiana,* from the West, is taller, 8–10 inches, and more upright in habit, with rather larger axillary white flowers, and is probably the species most amenable to cultivation. *C. tetragona* is another arctic kind of habit similar to *C. Mertensiana* and like it in that the flowers are axillary and the leaves arranged in a characteristic four-angled manner. The dainty *C. fastigiata* from the Himalayas has larger, almost ½-inch white axillary flowers, but is not so hardy as any of the foregoing.

CHAMAEDAPHNE. The species given here is the only one in the genus.

Chamaedaphne calyculata, "LEATHERLEAF." A very hardy circumpolar shrub, but not too imposing in the garden because of its small leaves and rather sparse shoots. About 3 feet tall, it has narrow leaves, reddish scaly beneath, to 2 inches long, which assume a brownish cast in winter that does not then add to the plant's appearance. But it is quite attractive in flower, as the drooping, leafy racemes, to 4 inches long with ¼-inch white, urn-shaped blossoms, are produced at the outer ends of the shoots in the axils of decreasingly smaller leaves. It will grow in boggy ground or acid garden soil. Rather more ornamental in appearance is the variety *nana,* which is less than half the above height and more densely branched.

CHIOGENES. Of the two small shrubs in this genus only the native one given here seems to be in cultivation. It is also known as *Gaultheria hispidula*.

Chiogenes hispidula, "CREEPING SNOWBERRY." A small trailing plant of northern North American evergreen woods and bogs, and another subject for shade in the rock or wild garden. The stems are clothed with bristle-like hairs, and the ⅓-inch alternate leaves are shiny on the upper surface, with a few stiff brown hairs beneath. The tiny, ⅛-inch white, nodding flowers occur in the axils of the leaves and are followed by white, aromatic, ¼-inch berries, which are the plant's most interesting feature. It is difficult of cultivation.

DABOECIA. There is only one small shrub in this genus.

Daboëcia cantabrica (*D. polifolia*), "IRISH HEATH." One of the showiest of the dwarf plants of the Heath family because of its larger individual flowers. Usually a foot or less in height, it has alternate, sharply pointed, shiny, dark green, ½-inch leaves, with white, fine, short hairs beneath. Flowers purple, as much as ½ inch long, urn-shaped, drooping, and rather loosely arranged on a raceme to 6 inches long, but longer in some of its varieties. Var. *alba,* with white flowers, is one of the prettiest; var. *atropurpurea* has longer racemes and is much brighter colored than the species; and in var. *bicolor* the flowers are mostly white streaked with purple, and usually other flowers are white or purple; var. *pallida* has pink flowers. A native of Spain and Ireland, *Daboëcia* has about the same degree of hardiness as *Bruckenthalia* and should be provided with a gritty, peaty soil and protection in winter such as is suggested for the latter.

EPIGAEA. The two creeping shrubs given here consititute the genus.

Epigaea repens, "TRAILING ARBUTUS," "MAYFLOW-

ER." This well-loved native of eastern North America has suffered much wanton destruction because its delightful fragrance has been the excuse for its wholesale collection for commercial sale. Too often, in order to obtain the flowering shoots, the whole plant was ripped out of the ground, a totally unjustifiable form of vandalism. Fortunately, some states now protect it by law, garden clubs prohibit its use in arrangements, and conservationists are exerting their efforts in every way to have it protected. It is a prostrate plant forming patches, most frequently in some shade, though it may also be found in sunny places. Leaves alternate, varying in size according to the conditions under which it is growing and to a lesser extent on the plant itself, to 3 inches long, and more or less coarse-hairy on both surfaces and the leaf margins. The bell-shaped flowers in small terminal clusters are white or a delicate pink, about ½ inch wide. Always difficult of cultivation, any attempt to establish it in the garden should be with pot-grown plants in a shady, well-drained location in an open soil made acid with peat moss, decayed Pine needles, or similar material. It is folly to attempt to establish plants taken from the wild. The similar Japanese *E. asiatica* is rare in cultivation and much less hardy.

ERICA, "HEATH." The hardy Heaths are pretty, small shrubs which, like *Calluna,* are more effective as points of interest when planted several together or in masses than as single plants. They require the same soil conditions as the latter, in sun or light broken shade. In areas away from the coast, they should be given a winter covering of evergreen branches or salt hay, at least until such time as they are thoroughly established. Most of the hardy kinds originate in western Europe— those from the Mediterranean region are generally too tender, and the South African species quite out of consideration for eastern gardens.

Erica carnea, "SPRING HEATH"

Erica carnea, "SPRING HEATH," is excellent, and the one most extensively planted, as it is hardy enough to take the winters without protection, except perhaps young plants, and it will tolerate a drier, less acid soil than most other species. Usually about 10 inches tall with linear leaves ¼ inch long which are arranged in rings of four around the stems. The flowers, of about the same length, are produced in the leaf axils on the upper part of the shoots, but all incline to one side of the shoot instead of being regularly arranged around it. They are deep pink to red, and normally begin to open in March or April, but mild, sunny weather in November and December will cause many of them to open at that time. There are now many varieties recognized in Europe, differing in the time at which the flowers open or their color, and though they are being gradually introduced here they are not too readily available. Alps of Central Europe.

Erica cinerea, "TWISTED HEATH." From western Europe, this is usually a plant to 1 foot or a little more in height, and with its flower color one of the daintiest Heaths. The young shoots are downy, and clusters of smaller leaves develop in the axils of the ¼-inch regular leaves, which usually occur in whorls of three around the stems. Flowers ovoid, purplish red, about the same length as the leaves, crowded on terminal racemes. The delightful *E. ciliaris,* Fringed Heath, from Southwest Europe and the British Isles is not sufficiently hardy for general planting, but its larger pink flowers, almost ½ inch long, on terminal racemes to 4 inches long, make it worth trial near the coast or where conditions favor the growth of Heaths.

Erica darleyensis. This hybrid, with *E. carnea* as one of its parents, is a taller plant than the latter, but neither quite so hardy nor showy, though it has the same soil tolerances. Except for its greater height and slightly smaller flowers it is almost identical with *E. carnea.*

Erica Tetralix, "CROSS-LEAVED HEATH." A rather loosely habited, spreading plant 1–1½ feet tall, and one of the hardiest and best. Covered with a fine down which gives it a grayish green appearance. Leaves about ⅛ inch long, arranged in four ranks along the stems, and ¼-inch rose-colored flowers.

Quite definitely gray in appearance is var. *mollis*, which has white flowers.

Erica vagans, "CORNISH HEATH." This plant makes a low mass of intertwined stems of a rather conspicuous light brown color. As in *E. carnea* the flowers occur in the axils of the leaves, but they do not appear until midsummer, do not crowd to one side of the shoots, and are smaller, paler, and pinkish purple in color. It is one of the hardiest.

GAULTHERIA. There are a number of Gaultherias, but only the two given below are of importance in northeastern gardens. Though some others are western natives they are difficult to obtain and little cultivated, and those from China and Japan are generally rather too tender.

Gaultheria procumbens, "WINTERGREEN." A dwarf, North American ground cover with underground stems from which simple shoots arise to about 4–5 inches. Each is topped by a few shiny, leathery leaves, to 1½ inches long, roughly oval in shape, with shallow, rounded teeth. Flowers small, white, drooping, which appear singly in the axils of the leaves and are followed by bright red, ⅛-inch berries which remain through the winter, but flowers and fruits are partly hidden by the leaves. It prefers partial shade, and may be used as an edging or ground cover for taller plants of the Heath family.

Gaultheria Shallon. A western species, usually requiring partial protection from winter sun and wind in the East. To 1½ feet or more in height, the shoots clothed with stiff bristles. It spreads by underground stems, and forms an attractive tall ground cover when used alone or in combination with still taller Ericaceous plants. Leaves broad-ovate, to 4 inches long, with small saw-like teeth. Flowers on 4-inch racemes which are clustered at the ends of the shoots, bearing ⅛-inch ovate white or pinkish flowers. The berries, about ½ inch across, are first purple, then black.

GAYLUSSACIA, "HUCKLEBERRY." Deciduous or evergreen shrubs, some with edible berries, though not of such good quality as the Blueberry, *Vaccinium,* which not infrequently is called Huckleberry.

Gaylussacia brachycera, "BOX HUCKLEBERRY." A small eastern North American plant of very local occurrence, 10–12 inches tall from underground creeping stems. Leaves alternate, oval, usually less than 1 inch long, thick and shiny, with small rounded teeth and tiny white or pinkish flowers borne on very short racemes in the leaf axils. It very rarely produces its blue fruits in the wild, and probably not at all in cultivation. Occasionally used as a ground cover. Huckleberry pie in restaurants is not Huckleberry but most frequently made of the fruit of one of the Vacciniums.

KALMIA. The Kalmias are all pretty in flower, and those given below are eastern natives. *K. latifolia* is the outstanding member and among the most beautiful of evergreen flowering shrubs, with the added satisfaction that it is perfectly hardy and always attractive in the Northeast if given suitable growing conditions.

Kalmia angustifolia, "SHEEP LAUREL," "LAMB-KILL." This very hardy North American shrub when in bloom does not approach in beauty its larger relative, *K. latifolia,* Mountain Laurel, and only to a limited extent finds a place in gardens, though it is well suited to a moist place in the wild garden. Normally to about 3 feet tall, it has narrow, lance-shaped leaves about 2 inches long, which are usually opposite on the shoots but sometimes in threes. The purplish red, basin-shaped flowers, ⅓ inch or a little less in diameter, are produced in clusters in the axils of the upper leaves of the shoots from the

Kalmia latifolia, "MOUNTAIN LAUREL"

previous year. The common name Lambkill derives from the belief that the foliage is poisonous to sheep.

Kalmia latifolia, "MOUNTAIN LAUREL." This native of eastern North America is probably familiar to every gardener living in the East, either as a very handsome garden shrub or as wild growth. When in bloom it is, without doubt, one of the most beautiful hardy evergreens, native or introduced. Commonly seen as a plant 2–6 feet in height, it may considerably exceed this size, particularly in its more southerly range. The alternate, rather thick, dark green, narrow-oval leaves, to 4 inches long, paler on the underside, give the plant a rather solid appearance, but its real beauty comes with the flowers. These are usually pink, though the shade varies from white to red, which may be due to environmental factors. Varietal names have been given to some of these color variations. The flowers come in dense clusters at the ends of the shoots, each flower basin-shaped, ¾–1 inch in width. It prefers a gritty, acid soil and will tolerate quite wet ground; and although in its native haunts it is often found on thin, rocky soils, when so located it does not always flower freely or regularly. The leaves are a darker green and the flowers last longer if it has the benefit of light shade.

Kalmia polifolia, "SWAMP LAUREL," "BOG LAUREL." Quite pretty when in bloom, this loosely branched little shrub is a good border plant in moist, acid soil but perhaps more fittingly accommodated in the wild garden. One–2 feet tall, it has two-edged shoots and narrow leaves, opposite or in threes, about 1½ inches long, shiny above and white beneath. The red flowers, several together, are terminal on the shoots and ½–¾ inch wide.

L E D U M . Ledums do not find much use as garden shrubs, probably because they are not so amenable to cultivation as some of the commoner Ericaceous evergreens. The dense brown felt on stems and the undersides of the leaves and their small, white, clustered flowers are their points of interest. A moist, acid soil is essential and some shade desirable, and they resent disturbance.

Ledum groenlandicum, "LABRADOR TEA." A small shrub to about 2 feet tall, or occasionally a little taller, and essentially a plant for moist, very acid soil. Leaves alternate, 1–2 inches long, and about half as wide, with down-turned margins, and the underside of the leaves and the young shoots densely covered with rusty brown, woolly felt. The dainty white flowers, to ½ inch in width, occur in crowded terminal clusters on the shoots. A native of the mountains and colder parts of northern North America.

Ledum palustre, "WILD ROSEMARY." Very similar to the foregoing but with rather shorter, to 1½-inch, still narrower leaves of about a quarter the width and a looser, more open habit of growth. *L. palustre* originates in the cold northern regions of Europe and Asia. It has no close relationship to true Rosemary *Rosmarinus officinalis.*

LEIOPHYLLUM. This genus now contains two species, because the plant more recently known as *L. buxifolium* var. *prostratum* has again been raised to specific rank and its former name, *L. Lyonii,* revived.

Leiophyllum buxifolium, "SAND MYRTLE." An upright, 1½-foot shrub, with smooth stems and leaves, the latter oval, about ⅓ inch long, and mostly alternate. Flowers white, each about ¼ inch in width, in crowded clusters on the ends of the shoots.

Leiophyllum Lyonii (L. buxifolium var. *prostratum),* "ALLEGHENY SAND MYRTLE." Much more prostrate in habit, with smaller, mostly opposite leaves. They are natives of Eastern states, and very pretty additions to a group of Ericaceous plants.

L E U C O T H O E . Of the evergreen kinds of *Leucothoë,* the eastern native, *L. editorum* (*L. Catesbaei*), if not the most beautiful in flower, is quite the hardiest. All have alternate leaves with finely toothed margins.

Leucothoë axillaris. This plant does not differ greatly from the more familiar *L. editorum,* but is from a lower elevation and a more southerly range in the eastern United States and consequently not so hardy. The leaves average less in length, to about 4 inches, are broader and more abruptly pointed than in *L. editorum,* and it is in no way superior to the latter.

Leucothoë Davisiae, from the West, is 2 feet or more in height. Leaves oval to 2½ inches long, blunt-pointed. Flowers drooping, white, ¼ inch long, in terminal and axillary upright racemes, 3–4 inches long. A very pretty shrub, but should be given protection in the North.

Leucothoë editorum (*L. Catesbaei*), "DROOPING LEU-COTHOE." A well-known shrub, native of the eastern United States, in common use in borders and foundation plantings as a plant 2–4 feet high, although in favorable locations it may be half again as tall. It is particularly suitable for shady positions, though when so placed the foliage will not assume such bright winter color as when more fully exposed to the sun. Leaves ovate-lanceolate, to 6 inches long, smooth, shiny, and drawn out to a point. They are dark green in summer, but the young expanding leaves and shoots are often most attractively reddish bronze in color, and in winter turn a deep purplish red. Flowers ¼ inch long, white, produced in drooping racemes, the longest racemes near the base of the flowering portion of the shoots, becoming shorter toward the outer end. Tht racemes are formed in summer, but at that time are compressed and the flower buds very small, and they assume a brighter color than

Leucothoë editorum, "DROOPING LEUCOTHE"

the leaves as winter approaches. The racemes do not elongate or the buds expand until the lengthening days of the following spring. A handsome shrub at any time of year because of the changes in foliage color, and also because of its flowers.

Leucothoë Keiskei. This species is from Japan, and has white, cylindrical, ½-inch flowers, larger than those of any *Leucothoë* previously described, in racemes about 1½ inches long, which arise from the ends of the shoots and the axils of their upper leaves. Leaves to 3 inches long.

L O I S E L E U R I A . Represented by the one small trailing plant given here.

Loiseleuria procumbens. A little shrub about 6 inches high, from the colder, northern portions of the globe. Its trailing stems root as they run, and it is suitable only for the rock garden. Leaves leathery, hardly ⅛ inch long, with down-turned margins, smooth above and white beneath, arranged in opposite pairs crowded on the stems. Flowers bell-shaped, pink or white, about ⅛ inch long, a few together in terminal clusters. An older name for this plant was *Azalea procumbens.* It is not very adaptable to a warm climate, and is usually difficult to establish.

P E R N E T T Y A . Of a number of kinds in this genus only the one given here appears to be in cultivation.

Pernettya mucronata. Particularly interesting for its brightly colored berries which persist all winter, but not sufficiently hardy for general planting in the northeastern area, though worth trial near the coast or further south. A shrub of a foot or more in height, spreading by suckers, with alternate, ovate, shiny, sharply pointed leaves to ¾ inch long. Flowers urn-shaped, white, about ⅛ inch long, which come in the axils of the leaves, and the berries red. There are, however, a great many varietal forms in which the color of the berries ranges from white to pink, red, lilac, or purple, and in size from peas to small marbles. Native to Chile and Magellan region.

PHYLLODOCE. The Phyllodoces are dwarf shrubs requiring rather special care if they are to be grown successfully. For most of them a cool, moist, shady place in the rock garden provides the most suitable environment. They all have alternate, linear, Heath-like leaves.

Phyllodoce Breweri, from the Sierra Nevadas, is under a foot in height, with leaves to ¾ inch long. Flowers saucer-shaped, purplish pink, ½ inch across, on short racemes terminal on the shoots.

Phyllodoce caerulea. A small shrub with crowded, spreading shoots, to 6 inches high, from the northern alpine regions of the world. Leaves linear, less than ½ inch long, with ⅓-inch, purple, urn-shaped flowers produced singly or a few together on slender stalks.

Phyllodoce empetriformis, from the West, is of approximately the same size as *P. caerulea,* but more upright, with rather longer leaves, and bell-shaped, rosy purple flowers produced singly in the leaf axils.

Phyllodoce glanduliflora, another western species, is almost twice as tall and has pale yellow flowers.

PIERIS. One native and one introduced species are among the most excellent evergreen shrubs for northeastern gardens.

Pieris floribunda, "MOUNTAIN PIERIS," commonly called Mountain Andromeda, is one of the best of hardy, evergreen, flowering shrubs. Usually 3–4 feet high, in its early years it is rather spreading in habit. Shoots with a coating of stiff hairs. Leaves alternate, ovate, to about 3 inches long, of a rather dull green, with a few teeth, and hairy on the margins. The 3- to 4-inch clustered, upright racemes are made up of many drooping, white, urn-shaped, ¼-inch flowers. It is native to the southern portion of the Allegheny Mountains. Considerably hardier than *P. japonica,* it lacks something of the grace of

Pieris floribunda, "MOUNTAIN PIERIS"

the latter and does not transplant so readily. It is worthy of notice that this shrub showed no evidence of injury in Yonkers, New York, after the exceptionally severe winter of 1933–34, and flowered profusely.

Pieris Forrestii, a Chinese species, is remarkable for the brilliance of its bronzy red young leaves and stems, the color being consistent and retained to a later stage of development than in *P. japonica*. Unfortunately, it is not satisfactorily hardy north of Washington, D.C.

Pieris japonica, "JAPANESE PIERIS," commonly called Japanese Andromeda. One of the choicer evergreens for border and foundation plantings, and beautiful at any period of the year. Usually a shrub 2–5 feet tall, and rather less in breadth, it may grow much taller in a suitable environment. Leaves alternate, glossy, about 3 inches long, usually widest above the middle, and as they unfold in spring often a beautiful reddish bronze, in striking contrast to the dark green of the older, mature leaves. The intensity of coloring, however, varies in different plants. The flower buds are formed in the summer on terminal racemes, and are conspicuous throughout the winter because of the reddish hue they assume with the approach of colder weather. With the increasing warmth of spring, the racemes lengthen to 4–5 inches and become fully pendulous, the buds increase in size and change from green to white, at which time they are ovoid and about ⅓ inch long. The length of the flower clusters, combined with the number of flowers they bear, and their very pronounced drooping habit give the plant a very graceful appearance. Though often grown where it is fully exposed to the sun, light shade is to be preferred, as there is always the possibility that the flower buds will be destroyed in winter by repeated freezing and thawing when in a sunnier position, and in the shade the plant is less subject to attack by lace bug.

Pieris japonica, ''JAPANESE PIERIS''

RHODODENDRON. This is a very large genus containing many hundred species, the vast majority of them too tender for cultivation in the East, though many are proving satisfactory in the milder Northwest.

Among hardy broad-leaved evergreens outstanding for the beauty of their flowers, there can be little doubt that Rhododendrons hold the highest place in popular esteem. In bloom they are magnificent, and for the remainder of the year their foliage, though it be small or massive, is usually decorative. Flower color ranges from white through pinks and reds to purples; yellow is represented only in some of the deciduous kinds, that is, the Azaleas, as the yellow-flowered evergreens, with one possible exception, are not hardy in the northeastern region. To the majority of the public in the eastern states the beauty of Rhododendrons is exemplified by a very few of the innumerable hybrid garden varieties grown in Great Britain and parts of Europe. These few, time has proved, are capable of withstanding a climate which, in its hot, bright summer weather and annual extremes of temperature, is far from ideal for these plants.

For the average homeowner, who is usually content to grow those Rhododendrons which may be expected to give the greatest return in beauty with the least worry about their hardiness, these tried and tested garden hybrids are the best. In all probability he will be unfamiliar with the differences in flower color of these varieties, so the most satisfactory method of deciding which of them to grow is to see them in bloom in good local nurseries and make a selection of those which are most pleasing to him, rather than to order indiscriminately the number of plants he requires and hope the flower colors will come up to his expectations.

Provided the soil is neither alkaline nor clay and there is a sandy or gravelly subsoil, most of the garden hybrids usually grown in the eastern area are tolerant of a range of soils, and often can be grown with very little extra soil preparation. However, any additional care in the way of adding organic materials is never wasted, and where a limited number of plants is to be used it is always advisable in order to obtain the best results.

Where it is proposed to make extensive plantings, observation of the behavior of Rhododendrons in nearby gardens or parks and inquiries among local nurserymen or from interested amateurs as to the need for special soil preparation in the district are advisable, as it may avert later regrets if it is not undertaken.

The following list contains some of the generally reliable hardy garden hybrids:

Album Elegans	pale pink
Album Grandiflorum	pale pink, fading white
Atrosanguineum	deep red, early
Boule de Neige	white, low plant
Caractacus	red
Catawbiense Album	white
Charles Dickens	red
Everestianum	lilac, frilled petals
Henrietta Sargent	deep rose
H. W. Sargent	crimson
Kettledrum	dark red
Lady Armstrong	light rose
Lady Grey Egerton	pale lilac
Mrs. Charles Sargent	rose red
Purpureum Elegans	purple
Purpureum Grandiflorum	purple, late
Roseum Elegans	rose, tinged purple

There is, however, another increasing group of enthusiasts who find their greatest satisfaction in persevering in attempts to grow the more uncommon wild or species Rhododendrons and the newer and more unpredictable hybrids. To them the pleasure derived from the blossoming of a Rhododendron of a kind not to be found in every garden far outweighs any satisfaction they may find in the massed beauty of a whole planting of hardier but commoner kinds. These devotees are a class by themselves, with their own organizations and publications, and the many species and hybrids under trial by its members cannot be dealt with here. It is enough briefly to mention below some Rhododendrons which have proved amenable to the northeastern region, depending upon the location in which they are grown and the care expended on them. On Long Island, New York, and in other gardens not far from the coast, a number of the improved English hybrids are being grown with considerable success, but further inland they should be tried experimentally in small numbers until it is evident they will tolerate a less favorable environment.

For species or hybrids about which there is little information as to their behavior, extra soil preparation should not be neglected. There should be no question of the necessary degree of soil acidity, or of its organic content, but even with these precautions their growth and blooming are unpredictable before they are given a trial. With some of them, annual growth and flower-bud formation may be satisfactory, but in any except the mildest winters the flower buds may be killed, an extremely discouraging occurrence when it happens year after year. As a measure of protection for both foliage and flower buds, they should be planted in positions sheltered from the coldest winds, where they are not directly exposed to winter sunlight, and added protection in the form of screens or complete enclosures may be required. Indeed, for the hardiest hybrids the greatest success is assured only when the force of the elements is modified.

Finally, it seems advisable to repeat again a piece of advice endorsed by all successful growers but too often disregarded by the inexperienced, namely, that the ground near Rhododendrons and related plants must not be dug over either for the destruction of weeds or the sake of appearance. Weeds should be pulled out by hand. As has previously been stated, Rhododendrons are surface rooting, and digging or hoeing will destroy many of these roots. If the plants are mulched to the full extent of the root spread or beyond, weeds will be a minor problem and the ground beneath a mulch remains soft and loose, permeable to water and air.

Neither North America nor Europe is rich in native kinds of evergreen Rhododendron, the majority of them coming from China, the Himalayas, and other parts of eastern Asia, and many of the introductions from those regions find the cooler, more equable climate of the coastal portions of the state of Washington and British Columbia much better adapted to their needs.

The Rhododendrons that follow vary in degree of hardiness; some are sufficiently hardy to cause no worry except in winters of more than normal severity, and others are satisfactory in milder areas. A few are included that are not entirely evergreen, that is, it is normal for them to lose more or less foliage every winter, apart from any loss due to particularly bad weather. These partially evergreen kinds are better known as Azaleas, consequently they really belong with those which are entirely deciduous and are not treated extensively here. But because these few are very decorative, the fact that they retain at least part of their foliage is the reason for including them. *Rhododendron indicum, R. mucronatum, R. obtusum,* and *R. yedoense* are examples, but unless otherwise noted the Rhododendrons given below are normally evergreen. With two exceptions, *R. racemosum* and *R. dauricum,* the flowers are produced from the terminal bud or buds at the ends of the shoots, with from one or two flowers to clusters of a great many from each bud.

In the two exceptions the flowers are axillary on the upper ends of the shoots.

Botanists now include the Azaleas with the Rhododendrons, so the old distinction which made the deciduous kinds Azaleas, with certain other characters, no longer holds. But the name Azalea is so well established in the pubic mind to distinguish the deciduous and, more recently, the semi-evergreen kinds from the evergreen that it will not be quickly discarded.

Rhododendron arbutifolium is an attractive hybrid, rather small, to 3 feet, of dense habit. Leaves to 2½ inches long, pointed at both ends, and scaly on the underside. The rosy flowers are about ¾ inch in width, in clusters. The flower buds are apt to winterkill in exposed situations.

Arnold Hybrids. These consist of a few very hardy evergreen Azaleas, but unfortunately, their purplish flower colors are not the most pleasing.

Rhododendron carolinianum. A native of North Carolina, and in gardens not often more than 3–4 feet tall. Leaves to about 3 inches long, smooth above, reddish scaly beneath. Flowers pink, 1½ inches across, several together. A very pretty, hardy plant which should be used more frequently in foundation plantings, in groups by itself, or in front of taller Rhododendrons.

Rhododenron catawbiense, "CATAWBA RHODODEN-DRON." A native of some of the southeastern states, and a rather smaller plant than the commoner *R. maximum,* Rose-bay Rhododendron. Usually to about 6 feet tall, though it may grow taller, but much more compact in habit and pleasing in appearance than the more openly branched *R. maximum.* Leaves to 4–5 inches long, rounded at both ends, with both surfaces smooth. There is some variation in flower color, but a purplish shade predominates which is not generally considered pleasing. There are many quite large flowers, to 2½ inches across, in each cluster. Though this species, because of its flower

Rhododendron catawbiense, "CATAWBA RHODODEN-
DRON"

Rhododendron dauricum.

color, is not common in gardens, it has been of immense value
to the hybridist, and enters into the parentage of the greater
number of excellent hardy horticultural varieties with greatly
improved color that are in much greater demand. Its variety,
alba, is one of the best hardy white Rhododendrons.

Rhododendron dauricum (*Azalea dahurica*) from eastern
Asia, usually retains some leaves through the winter. Its value
lies in its very early flowers which appear with the Forsythias.
Its hardy flower buds are seldom winter injured, though every
few years some of the expanded flowers may be blasted by late
frosts; but this is a risk worth taking in order to enjoy its early
blossoms. It is upright in growth, to about 5 feet. Leaves dark
green, to 2 inches long, blunt at the ends, and scaly beneath.
Flowers pale pink with a slight purplish cast, about 1½
inches in diameter, which occur singly in the upper axillary
buds on the shoots. The very similar but completely deciduous
R. mucronulatum seems to be somewhat hardier.

Rhododendron decorum, from western China, is proving to
be hardier than was anticipated, and is worthy of trial in a
protected position. Leaves 4–6 inches long, white beneath, with
some very small, scattered hairs, and white or pinkish flowers
about 2 inches wide.

Rhododendron ferrugineum, from the mountains of Europe,
is one of two known as Alpine Rose. A neat, 2- to 3-foot, dense
bush, with narrow, pointed leaves to 1½ inches long, red-brown
and scaly on the underside. Flowers pink, ½ inch wide, several
in each cluster.

Rhododendron Fortunei. A large-leaved and large-flowered
species from China that is being grown on Long Island, New
York, and should be suitable for similar mild sections. Leaves
6–7 inches long, with a short point and a rounded base.

Flowers pink or lavender-pink, fragrant, 3 inches wide. This is another species which has been of great value to the hybridist.

Gable Hybrids. Produced by Mr. Joseph B. Gable, who has made available a great number of hardy evergreen Azaleas. The growth habits of these hybrids vary considerably, and the colors are white, pink, and orange-red to purple. They are a very excellent group as a whole.

Glenn Dale Hybrids. Mr. B. Y. Morrison was the originator of this group, and he named them for the experiment station of the U. S. Department of Agriculture at Glenn Dale, Maryland. A great number of crosses were made and thousands of seedlings raised from the product, principally with the idea of providing the South Atlantic states with large-flowered Azaleas which would cover a long season of bloom. Though the majority of the clons, some with flowers 4 inches or more in diameter, will undoubtedly be best adapted to the region for which they were intended, some are proving to be hardy further north, and the group is well worth watching.

Rhododendron hirsutum shares with *R. ferrugineum* the name Alpine Rose, and is another European species differing only in minor characters from the latter, principally in the bristles on its shoots and leaf margins, but it is generally regarded as the better garden plant of the two. It is also of interest as growing in limestone areas in its native Alps.

Rhododendron indicum (*Azalea macrantha*). This Japanese species is usually a spreading, low shrub, almost entirely evergreen. Leaves to 1½ inches long, narrow, pointed at both ends, and with long scattered hairs on both surfaces. Flowers red, about 2½ inches across, one or two from each terminal bud. It is one of the showiest, as the bright flowers seem to be made more conspicuous because of the usually low stature of the plant, but winter protection may be necessary. Its attractive salmon-red, double-flowered variety *balsaminaeflora,* is very low in habit, usually keeping more or less close to the ground, but it is less hardy, which is also true of most of its many other varieties.

Rhododendron Keiskei. A Japanese species of interest as the hardiest of the yellow-flowered evergreen Rhododendrons, for though not reliably so, it is possible to grow it in the milder northern areas. The 2½-inch leaves are narrow-oblong, scaly and pale green beneath. Flowers pale yellow, about 1½ inches across, which occur in few-flowered clusters.

Rhododendron lapponicum. A very dwarf, arctic, or high mountain shrub of northern North America and similar climates in Europe and Asia, seldom as much as a foot high. Leaves to ¾ inch long, rough-scaly on the underside, as are the twigs. Flowers purple, ½ inch wide, in small clusters. It is a plant for some shade in the rock garden but is not easily grown, as it is intolerant of prolonged summer heat.

Rhododendron macrophyllum (*R. californicum*) from the West coast, does not seem adaptable to the East, and is most unsatisfactory. Flowers purplish pink, 2 inches wide, many in a cluster; and smooth leaves 4–6 inches long.

Rhododendron maximum, "ROSEBAY." Native to the eastern United States, this plant is common in northern gardens, and is the hardiest. Often a very large shrub, 10–12 feet, in the most favorable southerly gardens it may greatly exceed this size and become a small tree. With its looser, more open branching it is not so ornamental in appearance as the more compact *R. catawbiense,* nor are its flowers so large as those of the latter, but they are a much more pleasing color. Unfortunately, they do not appear until a considerable amount of new growth has developed, and this tends to hide the flowers. However, it is not negligible when in bloom, for though the flowers do not

Rhododendron maximum, "ROSEBAY"

stand out so prominently as those of showier hybrids, their partially hidden beauty cannot be overlooked. Flowers pale pink or nearly white, 1½ inches wide, many in each cluster. The leaves, sometimes as much as 8–9 inches long, taper to both ends, and are usually finely downy on the underside. Because of its size and hardiness, *R. maximum* forms a fine background for more tender or smaller kinds.

Rhododendron micranthum. This eastern Asiatic plant is noteworthy for the small size of the individual flowers on a shrub 3–4 feet tall. Leaves 1 inch or a little more in length, pointed at the ends, and brownish scaly on the underside. Flowers white, about ⅜ inch in width, crowded many together in the terminal clusters. It is among the hardiest, and an interesting if not particularly showy addition to a collection of Rhododendrons.

Rhododendron minus (*R. punctatum*). This plant is not very obviously different from *R. carolinianum,* though normally taller and with a more open manner of branching. The leaves average a little more in length, to 4 inches long, and its similar-sized flowers appear a little later. Of the two, *R. carolinianum* is to be preferred both for habit of growth and rather better flower color.

Rhododendron mucronatum (*Azalea indica* var. *alba, A. ledifolia* var. *alba, A. rosmarinifolia*), "SNOW AZALEA." This is another of the group not entirely evergreen, but is the outstanding white Azalea. Usually seen as a shrub 2–4 feet tall, it may be almost twice that height in the most favorable positions. Leaves dull green, to 2½ inches long, covered on both surfaces with gray hairs. Flowers pure white, 2½ inches or a little more across, which occur one to three together. Not one of the hardiest Azaleas, it is particularly subject to bark splitting and winterkilling as a young plant, but when it is beyond that stage, suffers injury only in severe winters, though the flower

Rhododendron mucronatum, "SNOW AZALEA"

Rhododendron hybrid, "EVERESTIANUM"

buds may occasionally be killed. Its beauty warrants any necessary winter protection. There are a number of varieties of it.

Rhododendron myrtifolium is a hybrid and a dense bush
2–3 feet tall. Leaves to 2½ inches long, brown scaly beneath,
and rather narrow. Flowers rose-pink, about ¾ inch across,
in clusters.

Rhododendron obtusum (Azalea obtusa). This species is
most frequently represented in gardens by its brilliantly colored
variety Hinodegiri, which is equally popular as a florists' pot
plant at Christmas and Easter. It retains most of its leaves

through the winter, and they assume a deep red as that season approaches. When the plant is covered with its myriad scarlet blossoms it is easy to understand why it is so heavily favored both for the quantity and the striking color of its flowers. It is no less true, however, that such extreme popularity sometimes leads to its excessive or inappropriate use. Readily propagated by summer cuttings, it begins to flower when very small, though plants 3 feet high, and more in diameter, are to be found in many gardens, and when in bloom they are solid mounds of scarlet.

Rhododendron obtusum var. *amoenum* may be a little hardier than Hinodegiri, but its magenta flower color does not harmonize with reds or pinks, though it is free-flowering and very effective when planted away from those colors. Leaves elliptic, about 1 inch long; and most of the flowers double (hose-in-hose), about ¾ inch wide. It holds a good deal of its foliage in winter.

Rhododendron obtusum var. *Kaempferi*, "TORCH AZALEA." This is the hardiest·of the varieties of *R. obtusum*, and entirely different in growth habit from its parent species, as for many years its principal shoots are upright, to 5–6 feet or occasionally more, so that the plant is rather sparse in outline until with increased age it begins to fill out and broaden. The leaves are 2 inches or a little more in length, and few if any of them persist through the winter, but it is included here because of its hardiness and showiness, which make it one of the most satisfactory Azaleas that may be grown in New England. The flowers are red, but there is a variation in its shade. It blooms quite freely when planted in considerable shade, and a certain amount is desirable, as the color fades all too quickly when it is fully exposed to the sun. There are a number of hybrid forms of it with white or pink flowers, but it is questionable whether any of them are as hardy as var. *Kaempferi*.

The Kurume Azaleas are derived from *R. obtusum,* but in the vicinity of New York City they are not reliably hardy. Their colors range from white through pinks, reds, and scarlet to magenta, some with double flowers. The thin bark of young plants is often split by frost and may be completely lifted off the wood; then the stems die. When they reach a size where this kind of injury is not such a serious threat, the flower buds are still particularly liable to winterkill. Many of them, however, make attractive pot plants, and they are usually safe outdoors in southern New Jersey.

Rhododendron ponticum is from Southwest Europe and Asia Minor and too tender for cultivation in the Northeast, and aside from this fault it is doubtful whether its purple flowers would meet general approval. It is commonly used as understock onto which better colored and hardier garden hybrids are grafted, but, by improved methods of propagation, increasing numbers of the latter are raised from cuttings or by layering as they are then on their own roots, which is to be preferred. In addition, all growth on plants raised from cuttings or layers is similar to the original shoot, whereas basal shoots on a grafted plant may be from the understock, and if they are not destroyed may eventually choke out the grafted variety, though fortunately they often winterkill.

Rhododendron racemosum. There appear to be two races of this Chinese Rhododendron in cultivation, one hardier than the other. The hardier one is a smaller, more compact plant; the other more loosely branched and of more upright habit. Leaves oval, 1 inch or a little more in length, with a white bloom beneath. Flowers pink, to 1 inch across and, unlike the majority of Rhododendrons, are not terminal on the shoots, but appear a few together in the axils of the upper leaves, giving the shoots a very distinctive appearance. Until its hardiness in a locality is assured, it is advisable to provide winter protection.

Rhododendron Smirnowii. A large shrub, 6–8 feet tall or taller, from the Caucasus, and one of the hardier large-leaved species. The young shoots and the underside of the young leaves are covered with a thick, felt-like growth of fine white hairs which later turn brown. This coating is occasionally mistakenly assumed to be a fungus growth, but it does have the merit of thwarting the injurious activities of the lace bug. Leaves to 6 inches long. Flowers deep pink, usually wavy edged, to 2½ inches across, in large clusters. It enters into the parentage of some of the hardy garden hybrids, but because of its color, hardiness, and good appearance should itself be grown more frequently.

Rhododendron yedoense (*Azalea yodogava*). This plant, from Korea, is nearly deciduous, and 2–3 feet tall, but much broader. It has very narrow leaves to 2½ inches long, with straight, long hairs flattened against both surfaces. Flowers pink, with a somewhat purple tinge, double, to 2 inches across, one to three from each bud. Though an old favorite, it is not now perhaps so widely grown as its hardier, more floriferous variety with single flowers, *poukhanense* (*Azalea poukhanensis*). This makes a larger plant and has pale lilac flowers. The latter particularly does not harmonize well with pink or red Azaleas.

RHODOTHAMNUS. One species represents this genus, which is very closely related to Rhododendron.

Rhodothamnus Chamaecistus (*Rhododendron Chamaecistus*). A handsome little shrub, rarely 1 foot in height, from the Alps. Leaves elliptic, ½ inch or less in length, and 1-inch-wide, Rhododendron-like flowers, pink with a purple center, produced two or three together from the buds. A rare plant because it is never easy to grow. It requires a position where its roots have the benefit of the coolness of a crevice in the rock garden.

VACCINIUM. A genus of many deciduous and some evergreen shrubs, including the popular and much cultivated Blueberry, *Vaccinium corymbosum,* as well as the Cranberries given here.

Vaccinium macrocarpon, "AMERICAN CRANBERRY." A bog plant suitable only for cultivation in sand and sphagnum moss in a wet place in the wild garden, and of little horticultural interest. Leaves alternate, oval, blunt at the ends, about ¾ inch long, on very thin prostrate stems from which the shorter flower-bearing shoots arise. Flowers pink, about ½ inch wide, followed by ¾-inch red berries which will persist through the winter. Principally in selected forms which are grown in carefully tended bogs, this plant is extensively grown in Massachusetts, New Jersey, and Wisconsin for its fruit, which is used by the ton for jellies and sauces.

Vaccinium Oxycoccus, "SMALL CRANBERRY." Very similar to the preceding, but with ½-inch, usually ovate, pointed leaves with down-turned margins, and a berry about half the size. It has the same cultural requirements and culinary uses as the larger kind. Both are North American plants.

Vaccinium Vitis-idaea, "COWBERRY." A low ground cover 8–9 inches high from a creeping rootstock. Leaves alternate, leathery, oval, about 1 inch long, covered on the underside with black, bristly dots; and ¼-inch, drooping, pink flowers in small clusters, followed by dark red, bitter berries, ¼ inch wide. This plant is from Europe and Asia, but the half size native North American variety *minus,* makes a denser growth and is a daintier little plant. Both are tolerant of a rather dry, peaty soil.

Glossary

Anther	The pollen-bearing organ of a stamen.
Aril	An extra covering of some seeds, often colored.
Axil	The upper angle formed by a leaf with a shoot.
Bract	A modified form of leaf often occurring below a flower or cluster of flowers, usually small and green.
Cladode	A leaf-like branch serving as a leaf.
Clon	The vegetatively propagated progeny of a single plant, never those increased by seed.
Compound (leaves)	With more than one blade, when they are called leaflets, on a common leafstalk; as in a pinnate leaf where the leaflets are arranged along the stalk, or a digitate leaf where the leaflets arise from one point at the top of the leafstalk.
Deciduous	Leaves, and other parts, that fall when mature, as the small shoots with attached leaves of some conifers.
Decurrent	With the leaf base extending down the stem.
Digitate	A compound leaf with the leaflets arising like fingers from the top of the leaf stalk.
Filament	The part of the stamen supporting the anther.
Glabrous	Smooth, without down or hairs.
Glaucous	With a bluish bloom.

Lanceolate	Like a spearhead, several times longer than broad, and tapering at the ends.
Leaflet	One blade of a compound leaf.
Linear	Long and narrow with almost parallel sides.
Lobe	Usually the rounded projections on the edges of some leaves.
Oblong	Twice or more as long as broad, with approximately parallel sides.
Obovate	Egg-shaped, with the narrow end at base.
Panicle	A compound raceme bearing flowers on the secondary branches.
Pinnate	A compound leaf with the leaflets arranged along a common stalk.
Pistil	The female part of a flower, composed of ovary, style, and stigma.
Pistillate	Having a pistil; generally used when there are no stamens.
Pollen	The usually dust-like grains produced by the anthers.
Raceme	A shorter or longer stalk bearing flowers, each attached by its own stalk.
Sepal	One of the divisions of a calyx.
Stamen	The male part of a flower, composed of filament and anther.
Staminate	Flowers with only male organs.
Stomata	Minute openings, usually most numerous on the under-surface of a leaf, for the exchange of internal and external gases and the discharge of water vapor.
Umbel	With the stalks of the individual flowers all arising from one point and of approximately the same length.

Index

Bold-face numerals indicate page references to principal descriptions.
Parentheses indicate rejected synonyms. Latin names in italics.

275

282